TRUE STORIES
of Elmira, New York

Volume 2

By Diane Janowski & James Hare

This book is a selection of their freelance articles
in the Elmira *Star-Gazette*

True Stories of Elmira, New York, Volume 2

ISBN: 978-0-9994192-1-2

Printed in the United States of America

First Edition

Cover image: Postcard view of Elmira, East Water Street from the Hulette Building. Published by the Acmegraph Co., Chicago.

Dedicated to new and future grandbabies!

Table of Contents

Babe Ruth Visits Elmira

by James Hare

I t was a busy week for Elmira. On Wednesday, October 17, 1928 Albert Ottinger, New York State Attorney General and Republican candidate for Governor spoke to supporters at a packed Colonial Theater. Two days later, Franklin D. Roosevelt, the Democratic candidate for Governor appeared before a huge crowd at Wisner Park.

Sandwiched in between these major political events, on Thursday, October 18, 1928 Babe Ruth and Lou Gehrig made a stop in Elmira as part of their post World Series barnstorm-

Babe Ruth in his first year with the New York Yankees, 1920. Photograph by Paul Thompson.

ing tour. The Yanks had swept the Cardinals. Ruth batted 625 with three homers and Gehrig drove in as many runs as the Cardinals did in the whole series. The Elmira *Advertiser* headline read, "Bambino Thrills Great Crowd...."

Schools were closed early so the students could see the Babe and Lou in action. The Yankee teammates would be managing and playing on opposing teams. The game would pit the Patch I. A. C. (Bustin Babes) against the Eclipse Machine Company (Larrupin Lous). Local players Mel

Kerr, Al Todd and Leo Casey among others would fill out the teams. Smokey Joe Genewich, Elmira's "contribution to the major leagues" returned for the visit.

Over 4,000 were expected at Dunn Field with 2,000 children being admitted free as guests of the promoter Myles G. Kelly. It was reported that "crippled children will be taken to the park in cars provided by Mr. Kelly." Following the game the promoter and the Babe were scheduled to visit the Rotary Reconstruction Home for Crippled Children to greet the "inmates" who were unable to make the game" (note: this home was founded by the Rotary, located at 563 Maple Avenue, the former home of Colonel Robinson, operated from 1923-37 and cared for over 350 paralysis victims).

There was great anticipation about the game. *Would he or wouldn't he was the question.* Sports reporter Glenn Sherwood wrote, "it has been said that no player living could clout a ball over the centerfield fence at the local park. Perhaps the Bambino will accomplish the feat."

The score was not close as the Babes beat the Lous 7-0. Gehrig had a single and double and Ruth hit a single, triple and delivered a tremendous 500-foot home run. According to the paper, "the sphere ascended skyward with a speed of a bullet after its' collision with the Ruthian war club and was still traveling upward as it went over the fence" landing on the roof of a house on Phoenix Avenue. It was something new to Elmira fans to see a runner jog around the bases after a home run since the wall was moved back. Ruth said it was "one of the longest drives I ever made." Following the game Ruth and Gehrig signed baseballs that were hurled across the diamond for their "youthful admirers" to retrieve.

Glenn Sherwood wrote about a special event after the game. "As the Babe and Gehrig were driving from Dunn Field to their hotel Ruth suddenly remembered that he hadn't visited the orphans' home (located on Franklin Street where the Marion Center is now).

So he instructed the taxi driver to take him there as quickly as possible. As Babe walked into the hall he was met by a group of delighted kiddies who recognized him instantly. Shrieks of delight greeted his appearance and the great star gathered the children around him and talked to them for almost half an hour. "You bet it is the little Babe himself" he said as he clasped the outstretched hands of the eager children, "and I am sure glad to see you kids."

Ruth had appeared in Elmira in 1923 after the Yankees had won their first World Series. He returned in 1938 after a two year break from baseball as a coach for the Brooklyn Dodgers. Five thousand fans were hoping to see a repeat of the 1928 homer. "I'm willing" he boomed at the Mark Twain Hotel. At the ballpark the fans cheered "lustily", reported the paper, when the Babe turned to the stands after his first few swings in batting practice failed to deliver a fence clearing wallup. "I'm not warmed up yet" he shouted and grinned while the fans went into a "frenzy of applause and shouts "come on bust one Babe." It was not to be. The Pioneers beat the Dodgers 3-2.

AMERICAN GIRL AND LADY THORN.

A Currier and Ives print of *American Girl*.

ELMIRA DRIVING PARK
ASSOCIATION.
—
INAUGURAL MEETING,
SEPT. 28, 29, 30 & OCT. 1, 1875.
—
PREMIUMS - - $10,500.

This Association will inaugurate their new track during the week of the New York State Fair, to be held at Elmira. The track is but a few rods distant from the Fair Grounds, and adjoining Eldridge Park; is 75 feet wide, turns easy, and, with its hotel, stands, stabling, etc., is first-class in all its appointments.

The newpaper advertisement for the races, September 28, 1875, Elmira *Telegram*.

American Girl Race Horse

By Diane Janowski

$20,000 was riding on *American Girl,* the most famous racing trotter in the country, on October 2, 1875 right here in Elmira.

The Elmira Driving Park Association formed in 1874 to support and promote the sport of horse racing. Their half-mile track was on a 30 acre lot along Grand Central Avenue. The inaugural week of racing on the track was September 28 – October 1, 1875 with a "Free-for-All" race on October 2.

Bay-colored *American Girl* was born in 1862 in Peekskill, New York. "Weak-jointed, loose-gaited, worst looking, crooked-legged filly that was ever foaled in Peekskill," but grew into an outstanding specimen of a "Standardbred" horse. She was owned by William Lovell, of New York City, and was valued at $25,000. *American Girl* raced between 1868-1875 and won 52 races. 1875 started well, but she had only won one race.

On the morning of the race, thirteen-year-old *American Girl* was believed to be feeling well after recovering from a "prevailing epizootic." She was driven by John L. Doty, and appeared at the start to be in the very best condition. The horses were scored a number of times before they got the word to race. *American Girl* at the first turn was well ahead. At this point her driver noticed that she seemed to be giving out, and let her head loose. She kept staggering for an eighth of a mile, and at the quarter-pole fell and died instantly without a struggle. She fell very easily, with her shoulder against the fence. The incident excited a great deal of sympathy, as the mare was a favorite in Elmira, and had been the chief attraction for that race. A slight rain was falling and the western sun formed a very clear and distinct rainbow.

It was determined to bury *American Girl* near the spot where she died. The Elmira Driving Association erected a $2,500 monument to her memory. The handsome bronze monument was first located across the road from the east entrance to Eldridge Park on Grand Central Avenue.

In 1883, the Delaware, Lackawanna & Western Railroad ran a line through Eldridge Park splitting the park in half. Remaining to the east was the race track, and to the west stood the first-class Park View Hotel (still standing at the northern end of Eldridge Park). Access to the driving park was made difficult by the rail line. When the race track portion of Eldridge Park was abandoned, the *American Girl* monument was moved west of the railroad track. It was broken by vandals in 1980.

There were many fast horses locally but racing popularity dwindled. The last official race at Eldridge Park was about 1880. The last time the track was used was 1883 when Buffalo Bill brought his Wild West show to Elmira during the New York State Fair.

The grounds reverted to a swamp after the abandonment of the race track, and had turned into a haven for gypsies and squatters. Today a paved path leads from Eldridge Park to Lake Street, home to turtles, herons, kingfishers, and muskrats. Half way through, visitors can take the northern path along the remains of the Chemung Canal.

Sources:

Elmira *Gazette*, May 6, 1907
Elmira *Daily Gazette* Feb 6, 1900
The Telegram, January 26, 1919
New York *Spirit of Times* 1875
Watkins Glen *Democrat* June 7, 1876
New York *Evening Express* October 4, 1875
Elmira *Morning Telegram* about July 15, 1907

Billy Sunday's Revival in Elmira

by James Hare

Billy Sunday preaches circa 1910.

Billy and "Ma" Sunday arrived in Elmira on September 13, 1924 the day before his six week revival was to begin. They were greeted at the train station, where Billy worked the crowd, then taken to the Langwell Hotel where they would reside while in Elmira. Preparations had been underway for some time. Thirty-seven Protestant churches and the Salvation Army were supporting the revival. The Tabernacle was located on the corner of Clinton Street and Park Place. It could seat 8,000 of the faithful. There would be three services on Sunday and two every other day of the week but Monday. Staffing would require 500 ushers and 150 secretaries to handle the paperwork of commitment. The choir would number 800 singers.

According to the Elmira *Advertiser*, Billy Sunday was "the originator of the most dramatic type of religious service ever introduced to the American people. Turning from professional baseball (1883-1890) he has become one of the most sensational evangelists of the world." He was ordained a Presbyterian minister in 1903.

On September 14th the "greatest religious revival in the history of the city" opened. Congressman Gale Stalker (39th District) "pinch hit" for the mayor. He welcomed Sunday at the morning service pointing out that "we believe in law enforcement including the 18th amendment. I am proud to tell you that there are no breweries operating in this district..." Mounting a chair after being introduced, with one foot high on the pulpit, Sunday shouted at the top of his voice, "I am here to drive the devil out of Elmira," and 8,000 men and women, filling the Tabernacle to capacity yelled their approval. More than 20,000 people heard him preach that first day.

Newspaper coverage was extensive. All of his sermons were printed daily in both the *Gazette* and *Advertiser*. He preached 79 different sermons. It was estimated that over 400,000 people attended by the close of the revival on October 27th. He excoriated the whiskey gang. "I intend to make it so dry you will have to prime a man before he can spit." He had competition while in Elmira. "Al Smith is coming to Elmira. You Democrats know just what he is going to say. Teddy Roosevelt is coming to Elmira and you Republicans know just what he is going to say. You'd better come here to hear me for you DON'T know what I'M going to say." On student night over 3,000 young folks from Elmira Free Academy, Southside, Elmira Heights and Horseheads High Schools attended with their cheer leaders. Sunday urged them to, "look forward young people! Aim high." He held a service for men preaching about "When the Chicks Come Home to Roost."

The Tabernacle had a large carpeted platform several feet above the ground. The "sawdust trail" led from every section of the huge building to the platform from which Sunday preached. He would stride from side to side and "flay" the forces of evil. He would tap the alter with his forefinger, strike it with his fist and would bring down his "clenched right hand with sufficient force to make the electric lamp fixtures ring and jingle." Dripping with perspiration he would invite the faithful to "Get Right With God" and hit the sawdust trail. Men and women would "hit the trail" which covered the ground several inches deep. A trap door on the platform would open and Sunday would descend a set of stairs to an opening in front where he would shake the hands of the repenting sinners as they came down the trail. 6,336 men and women made the trip.

Approximately 40,000 attended the four services on the last Sunday. On the platform there was a basket of white chrysanthemums, a gift of the Ku Klux Klan. Mr. Sunday stated that he welcomed the friendship of any organization that stood for Christ. When the Sunday party said farewell at the Erie station 1,500 faithful sang "God Be With You Till We Meet Again".

In a farewell letter to the city, Billy Sunday wrote, "I've reveled in the historical interests that clusters about the Queen City of the Southern Tier... God seems to have set Elmira like a jewel in a marvelous setting."

Dreams of Freedom

by Diane Janowski

First page of the Newtown (now Elmira) census of the Tioga (Chemung) County 1810.

In 2002, I had the opportunity to work for James Loewen, sociologist, and professor of race relations at the University of Vermont, and author of *Lies Across America,* and *Lies My Teacher Told Me.* He was finishing a book called *Sundown Towns* and needed information about African Americans in Elmira in the early 20th century.

I had to look up what a "sundown town" was. It means a town that is "white on purpose." This idea dated from around 1900 to 1950. According to his census research about Elmira, West Elmira in particular, he believed it to be a sundown town. Wikipedia says in sundown towns "restrictions were enforced by some combination of discriminatory local laws, intimidation, and violence." Some towns had posted signs stating that people of color were allowed to be in the town limits in the daytime, but had to be out by sundown.

My first reaction was "Of course not. Not in my Elmira." But, I thought of Loewen's book. Maybe I am naïve. He claimed he could tell from census records, which towns were and were not, sundown towns, and West Elmira fit his criteria. In other towns, people did remember the signs and the rules. So, I started asking people who were alive in the 1920s and 30s if this was true, or if they had ever heard about sundown rules locally, or remembered the signs. I asked twenty older people, and they all said, "No." I looked in old newspapers. Nothing. I relayed my information to Mr. Loewen, and probably because of me, Elmira is not listed in his book. It is however listed as a "possible" sundown town on his website.

In Elmira today, we are proud of our abolitionists – those who fought locally to end slavery between 1830 to 1860, whether by speech or by act. We honor those who helped along the Underground Railroad. Because it was illegal to help escaped slaves at the time, it is hard to know today exactly what happened. We have legends. The Friends of Wood-lawn Cemetery website has an interactive map to learn about our local abolitionists. The John W. Jones Museum highlights the history of local African Americans, and the activity of local abolitionists.

What we don't talk about in Elmira are our slave owners and slaves. In the 1800 census, race designations where "white," "slave," or "free colored persons." Locally, four prominent citizens owned 3 slaves, and housed 5 free colored persons. In 1810, eleven Elmirans owned 13 slaves. In 1820, seven slave owners listed 12 slaves, and 9 free colored persons.

Prominent residents were local slave owners. Included were: a Presbyterian church officer, a town clerk, a highway commissioner, several farmers, a state senator, a justice of the peace, a school commissioner, a judge, and more.

New York State abolished slavery in 1827, and the 1830 census listed 43 free persons of color. 1840 showed 110 free persons of color in Elmira. 1850 showed 248 persons of color in Elmira, including John W. Jones who arrived in 1844. Beginning in 1850, the census designated three races – white, black, and mulatto. "Free colored person" was no longer an option. After the end of slavery, many white residents continued to house former slaves and kept their employ as servants.

In 1837, the first Methodist Conference of Western New York gathered in Elmira. As the city council forbade the meeting at the church or courthouse for fear of "creating a disturbance," it was held on Clinton Island in the Chemung River near the foot of Washington Street where there was no jurisdiction. It was an opportunity for those who were anti-slavery to express their views. Thomas Stanley Day accepted those who felt the same way into his home on East Washington Avenue for their church services. This was one the early schisms with local churches and eventually forty people founded the Independent Congregational Church in 1846.

A young male slave, born in 1817, dreamed of freedom on the Mount Middleton plantation outside of Leesburg, Virginia – near the runway of today's Dulles Airport. Years later in 1885, this same man – John W. Jones - told an Elmira *Telegram* reporter that he did not attempt to escape until his elderly owner "had given up the personal management of her estate." John said, "After the death of Miss Elzy, they would all probably be separated by sale into different families, and that he resolved at an early day to take his two half-brothers and run away."

In June 1844, John told his mother that he was "going to a party" to spare her the pain of parting. That night at 10:00PM, John, his two brothers, and two men from a neighboring plantation started walking north. The first night they walked eighteen miles. Before starting out, they "swore to fight to the death, and never to surrender." Each man carried a pistol.

On July 4, the group reached Troy, Pennsylvania during a parade. The large crowd scared the men so they continued walking for fear of slave catchers. At a farmhouse at South Creek, a farmer asked them whether they were hungry. After never having an invitation into a white person's house - they gladly went inside. John recalled to the *Telegram* that hot biscuits and butter had never tasted so good.

The next morning the group reached Elmira "where they made their first stop since their escape," and all settled down for a good rest. According to "Uncle John" Smith's obituary in 1898, they also changed their names for their personal safety. John W. Jones, George W. Jones, Charles Jones, John Smith, and Jefferson Brown walked into Elmira as free men.

John arrived at the Lake Street bridge with $1.56 in his pocket when he paid a 2-cent toll for each of the men to cross. The same day he made his first 50-cents by chopping wood for Mrs. Culp (daughter of pioneer John Hendy) on Lake Street. He said she knew he was an escaped slave, and she told him about when her father first brought her to Elmira.

The *Telegram's* article concludes with John's quote, "My life, as I look back over it, seems to me a wonder of wonders. Here, I am at sixty-nine, but I do not feel like an old man - free, happy, prosperous, at least have enough to eat, yet I was once a slave, and that time seems as if it were but yesterday, so distinctly do I remember the old life."

Sources:

Elmira *Telegram* January 3, 1885 "Slavery To Freedom - The Life of John W. Jones, Once a Slave, Now a Rich Citizen"

Elmira *Telegram* April 16, 1898 "Uncle John Smith"

The John W. Jones Story by Barbara Ramsdell

US Federal Census records 1800, 1810, 1820, 1830, 1840, 1850

Life in Black & White: Family and Community in the Slave South. By Brenda E. Stevenson. (New York: Oxford University Press, c.1996.

Will of Miss Sarah Ellzey, 8 October 1840. Virginia Historical Society

History of Tioga, Chemung, Tompkins, and Schuyler Counties, New York p 222

http://sundown.afro.illinois.edu/sundowntownsshow.php?id=229

Coconut Bowl

by James Hare

The possibility loomed that the "Elmira High Schools" might find themselves without football opposition "during the 1936 season." The New York State Public High School Athletic Association had ordered the local schools (Elmira Free Academy and Southside had a combined football team) "suspended for one year, if the post-season game at Miami (the Coconut Bowl) was played on Christmas Day (1935)." According to the rules, "no school may compete in a post-season football game after Saturday following Thanksgiving Day." Elmira was not a member of the Association, but all of its opponents for the 1936 season, but one, were. The Association "black listed" Elmira, but the sentence was "deferred indefinitely."

The 1935 football season for the Elmira High School team was one of the great seasons in Elmira sports history. In this "undefeated" season of seven games, Elmira totaled 173 points compared to only 18 for their opponents. The record made them early favorites for the Coconut Bowl. Winning the invitation was not "without drama." The Miami committee had before its consideration 92 schools representing 21 states. According to a committee member, five governors had entered pleas for their respective candidates.

News of Elmira's selection reached the *Telegram* by telegraph and a telephone call and reported December 8th. On December 18th the Elmira *Advertiser* reported that, "for the sixth time in as many years Miami High will represent Florida in the annual Christmas Day intersectional high school football classic." A game described as the "Rose Bowl" game of high school football.

There was excitement in the city about the trip to Miami. It was felt that it would be a great value from an advertising standpoint and local sponsors decided that the players must make the trip in "the best possible style." Plans were made to charter a Pullman car for the entire journey. The cost of the trip was approximately $3,000, with Miami picking up one third, leaving the local community to raise $2,000. Twenty-six lettermen were eligible for the trip. Service clubs stepped up, a tag day sale downtown was organized and a benefit dance at the Majestic Ball room was held to raise funds.

At a cost of $250, it was decided to purchase new uniforms for the team as it, "would be impossible for them to play in their old suits in the warm Florida climate." A program of entertainment was planned for the players while in Miami including deep sea fishing, golf and a banquet in their honor.

Twenty-five players, coach Al Hirst, trainer Doc Kittle, Ted Huntley, Howard Tryon and others composed the party headed for Miami. A crowd of Elmirans gathered at the Pennsylvania station to see the team off at 11:05PM on Friday night December 20th. The train would arrive in Washington D.C. at 7:55AM Saturday, with a scheduled workout at Georgetown University. They would travel two more nights before reaching Miami.

The boys lived "the life of Riley" on the train. They were so well fed and comfortable that it worried coach Hirst. With temperatures in the teens and three to four inches of snow in the Carolinas the boys wondered, "is our train headed the wrong way?" All was not roses as player Jim Cunningham "confided he was cold at night. Jim was too long for his berth. Wrapping covers around his shoulders, his feet were exposed...." In Washington, the train car with the cases of Chemung water was situated thirty miles away, but was rescued by the assistant general passenger agent accompanying the party.

When the team arrived in Miami a "memorable incident occurred. More than a dozen girls—apparently given the assignment on merits of personal charm—surrounded the bus. All were beauties, chic in summer garb. And immediately the boys went to work. Dates were arranged on the spot—for after the game of course." The team stayed at the Casa Loma Hotel in Coral Gables.

The team arrived on Monday evening (23rd) with a long workout on the Miami field scheduled for Tuesday. Glen Sherwood, Sports Editor for the Advertiser, alerted Elmirans that the game would be broadcast on WESG with "Bill Pope and Glover Delaney recreating the play by play story," just as it was played.

Coverage of the game began at 2:30PM on Christmas Day. Sherwood reported that more than 7,500 spectators saw the game, "and at least 7,250 of them were rooting for Miami." It was the "Light Blue" of Elmira versus the "Stingarees" (sic) of Miami, in the seventh Cocoanut Bowl. The game was a thriller.

In the opening two minutes, Harry O'Neil, the Elmira fullback, playing defense, intercepted a Miami pass carrying it 24 yards to the Miami 41. On the next play, halfback Walter Zimdahl, broke free to cross the goal line standing up. James Cunningham's kick was wide. Twice the Elmira defense would hold the Stingarees (sic) in the "shadow of their own goal." Near the end of the game O'Neil intercepted another pass, returning it to Miami's 13. Zimdahl scored four plays later and the kick was good. Elmira won 13-0.

The day after the game all twenty-five players went deep sea fishing in a forty foot boat at Seven Keys, fifteen miles from Miami. The coach's son, Jack Hirst, caught a three-foot snub nosed shark and no one got seasick. It was reported that "James Moylan, Bill Murphy and Jim Cunningham convulsed the party with an impromptu funny sketch."

Upon returning to Elmira, one event was scheduled to honor the team. It would be a banquet held at the Elks Club on January 11th. Only

THURSDAY, DECEMBER 26, 1935 _____ELMIRA STAR-GAZETTE_____PAGE FIFTEEN.

Miami Fetes Triumphant Elmira High Schools Squad

Elmira *Star-Gazette* headline December 26, 1935, page 15

300 tickets would be sold. School officials felt that only one big event should be arranged for the team, with Regents exams only two weeks away.

Frank F. Tripp was master of ceremonies. The victory ball, used in the game, was given to Clinton Williams (who was unable to travel to Florida because the Coconut Bowl would not allow "coloreds" but, "had the promise of the team that it would return with the pigskin for him.") In his remarks, Tripp said:

"We cheer you for your victories but we remind you that those victories always came through another's defeat and placed upon you the responsibility of good sportsmanship which is best exemplified in being a humble winner... More than the score you brought back from Miami we thank you for the reputation for manliness which you left down there. We are proud that you made the word, "gentlemen" synonymous with Elmira in the Southland."

Elmira Teall, Woman of Mystery

by Diane Janowski

According to legend, Captain Nathan Teall came to Newtown (now Elmira) around 1794 and opened Teall's Tavern on Sullivan Street near East Water Street. One of the frequent guests was State Assemblyman Judge Emmanuel Coryell who lived somewhere between Athens and Owego. At the time Judge Coryell was head of a committee to change the name of Newtown as there were several other Newtowns in the state.

According to the *Star-Gazette* on June 27, 1939, *"One night in 1806 little Elmira Teall, Nathan's youngest daughter climbed into his [Coryell's] lap and went to sleep. Noticing her beauty, Judge Coryell thought it matched the beauty of the surrounding country and later according to the story asked for the Board of Trustees to change the name of Newtown to Elmira. The name Elmira is said to come from Spanish words of Moorish origin 'El Mira' meaning beautiful outlook.' Wellington's troops took the name back to England from their Spanish campaigns, and eventually it became the name of a character in a book. It is surmised that Mrs. Teall had read the book and named her youngest child after that character."*

But who was Elmira Teall, and what's her story? I had to do some detective work.

The Tealls lived in Elmira until around 1805 when they moved to Horseheads with their five daughters and four sons. Shortly thereafter they moved to Watkins Glen. The Tealls operated a tavern at the foot of Seneca Lake near today's Harbor Hotel. It was a popular spot for tourists who traveled around Seneca Lake. Visitors stopped at Teall's Tavern for "a glass of their favorite wine or one of those "slings" fashionable at the time." The October 30, 1894 Geneva *Advertiser* described Nathan Teall as a "jovial landlord with a hearty welcome to greet the coming guest, and just as cheery a goodbye to speed the departing guest. Mrs. Polly Teall was a model landlady."

The Teall family left Watkins Glen for the Widner farm in Waterloo, New York in 1810.

Nathan and Polly Teall's gravestone in Geneva's Washington Street Cemetery. Photo courtesy of Mark Gossoo.

So, then I started a genealogy of Elmira Teall. According to the Chemung County Historical Society, they believe Elmira was Phoebe Elmira Teall who became Phoebe Madden, wife of John Madden. But, I'm not so sure this is correct.

The *Star-Gazette* article mentioned above says "youngest daughter." My research shows that Nathan and Polly had three daughters before the Newtown name change meeting. Elmira was born on December 20, 1795, Phoebe was born on June 24, 1797, and Sarah E. was born November 10, 1799. These three birth dates are important because according to their brother, Horace Nathan Teall, in a published letter to the Geneva *Advertiser* on April 18, 1881, he stated that his father "from 1792 bought several lots from Moses DeWitt in Dewittsburg, afterwards called Newtown, and later Elmira. The latter name was for my sister, started by Mathew Carpenter, and other friends of the family at Nathan Teall's Inn on said farm, at a meeting held there called for the purpose of changing the name of Newtown to some other name. They had met there several times but could not agree. As my sister, then about four-years old, and a great favorite of all (both whites and Indians) went running into the room, she was caught up and held up, and her name rang out *ELMIRA*, amid the cheers and clapping of hands; that decided the name of the town."

Brother Horace claimed this was 1800 (the *Star-Gazette* says 1806) as he had his father's letter when Mr. Carpenter appointed Nathan to public office shortly after the Elmira name decision. So, the first daughter Elmira would have been around five-years old, Phoebe would have been around three-years old, and Sarah, theoretically, would have been too young for this legend if Horace were correct. So, now I narrow it down to these two older sisters.

As a genealogist, I can make several possible surmises on what happened to Elmira Teall. According to the family tree I made, she was born in the Western Reserve, Connecticut in 1795 – this was actually a piece of northeastern Ohio that had been claimed by Connecticut, and called Connecticut. From there, I find no trail between this Elmira and the rest of the family. Many of the Teall family are buried in the Washington Street Cemetery in Geneva, but not Elmira Teall, nor anybody else named Elmira.

Could Elmira have possibly died between 1795 and 1797, and the family named the next daughter Phoebe Elmira as was a popular custom. Or, did she live and just was not mentioned again, and if not, why not. I did not find a maiden aunt living with any of the Teall nieces or nephews in New York State censuses from 1730-1750. The closest possibility I found was an Elmira Lamphere who was born in 1795 in Connecticut, and lived in Waterloo, New York at the same time as the Tealls, but I did not find any connection to the Teall family. I did not find this Elmira's husband or burial either.

I found six women named Elmira who were born in, or around, 1795 in Connecticut, or New York, none of which seem to fit.

After I finished my version of the Teall family tree, I found and corresponded with a woman who is in the current generation of the Teall family. The family tree she created on Ancestry.com is similar to mine – with sisters Elmira and Phoebe being two separate people. Her birth dates on these two sisters were slightly different from mine. She also has no further listings of either sister after their births.

Someday, I may have an updated story to tell about Elmira Teall, but until then I consider her a mystery.

Sources

Ancestry.com

Teall Family Tree http://tinyurl.com/pnnjgup

Elmira's Third Public Charity

by James Hare

In 1876, Francis Murphy began his temperance movement in Pittsburgh, Pa. He had 65,000 people sign the following pledge after he first spoke there. "With malice toward none, with charity for all, I hereby pledge my sacred honor that, God helping me, I will abstain from the use of all intoxicating liquors as a beverage and that I will encourage others to abstain." At the end of March 1877, perhaps stimulated by President Rutherford B. Hayes and his wife "Lemonade" Lucy occupying the White House, the "Pittsburgh Crusade" came to Elmira. Mr. Eccles Robinson, Crusade Leader, identified the keynote of the campaign as "love, love to the drinker, love to the seller...."

The *Daily Advertiser* reported on April 2, 1877, "The meeting at the Opera House... was one of the grandest and most inspiring demonstrations...it has rolled up a wave of popular enthusiasm and faith which will break down all resisting forces and accomplish miracles in the regeneration of our city." Meetings were held throughout the city. On Monday, April 9th, the *Advertiser* noted, "it is said of Methodists that they never half do anything. This remark could certainly be applied to the South Main Street Methodist Episcopal Church yesterday, for it was sign the Murphy pledge all day long."

The Crusade continued into June. Francis Murphy came to Elmira a number of times and over 6,000 people took the pledge. The Elmira Ladies Temperance and Benevolent Union was formed in May establishing a headquarters on the corner of Lake and Carroll Streets over the Bundy Brothers' store. Perhaps most importantly "The Industrial School," which Ausburn Towner described as "the third most extensive public charity in which the citizens of Elmira have reason to take pride," (Orphans' Home, and Home for the Aged were the first two) emerged as a result of the Murphy Movement. There was a desire "to assist the families

WOMEN PLANNING FOR FAIR FOR THE INDUSTRIAL SCHOOL

Will Be Held Next Week Thursday and Friday—List of Those Who Are Taking Active Part in the Work and Have Charge of the Booths.

Headline in the *Star-Gazette* (Elmira, New York) November 25, 1907 page 4.

of the pledge-takers and help the pledge-takers themselves in keeping their newly formed resolutions."

As temperance enthusiasm lessened interest in the school grew. In 1879, a little house at 107 West Second Street was acquired. A small sewing school was established to teach both black and white women how to use the sewing machine and besides the teaching, each child who attended was given a warm meal. It met with such success that in July 1883 the cornerstone for a new building at the corner of Church Street and Madison Avenue was laid. Mrs. William E. Knox spearheaded the project and Mrs. Mariana Arnot Ogden gave "upwards of $5,000" to solidify the finances. The school was governed, similar to the other public charities, by a committee of ladies of several churches and an advisory board of gentlemen. The *Telegram* reported the total cost for ground, building and furniture was $14,266.40.

The purpose of the Industrial School was to "gather into such school vagrants and idle children... to teach the rudiments of learning in different branches of industry... to instruct the thriftless of all ages in sewing and other industrial pursuits and a Biblical knowledge... to visit and instruct the poor generally...." With the opening of the school, a city missionary was appointed whose duty was to visit the poor and distressed. The annual report published July 1, 1894 indicated 100 students enrolled (56 boys, 44 girls) with 9,745 meals furnished and 1,401 pounds of food distributed. Classes were conducted in carpentry and design, cooking and sewing. According to the *Telegram* "children were taught neatness, punctuality, politeness and honesty." County Historian Tom Bryne noted that in 1908 the Industrial School was consolidated with the Social Service League and the red brick building became the Odd Fellows Temple.

The consolidation led to a need to move into the poorer sections of the city. "Two small rooms on Hatch Street next to the old rolling mill property and another small room or two on Dickinson Street" became centers from which "radiated the spirit of neighborliness and where kindergartens were daily held" according to the *Telegram* on November 25, 1923. The centers were open to "all nationalities and creeds, where patriotism was the watchword and good citizenship the goal." Eventually the programs were combined in a vacant butcher shop at the corner of Fifth and Dickinson Streets. This proved inadequate so "a large assembly room or gymnasium was built, where there could be held picture shows, dances, shows, parties... all kinds of gymnasium work and games."

From this beginning emerged the Neighborhood House. The original program was incorporated under the name of the Elmira Industrial School Association and it was changed on January 11, 1911 to the Elmira Industrial School and Free Kindergarten. On December 1, 1926, by a certificate filed in the Department of State, the Elmira Neighborhood House, Inc. officially came into existence.

Elmira's 150th Birthday

by Diane L. Janowski

The year 2014 marked Elmira's 150th anniversary of becoming a city. Elmira Downtown enjoyed marketing our history in fun ways throughout the year.

By the time that Elmira had become a full-fledged city in 1864, much of its important history had already happened. Newtown, eventually renamed Elmira, was settled and organized into a village-like semblance. As early as the 1790s, Newtown had already constructed justice buildings, houses of worship, merchants, blacksmiths, etc. In its early days, residents of Newtown were white, Protestant, immigrants from New England.

Elmira had struggled through the construction of the Chemung Canal in 1833 – a feat that opened the regional manufacturing trade to the world, and brought the influx of German and Irish immigrants. They were also, for the most part, Catholic. Elmira was not accustomed to newbies, an "us vs. them" mentality developed that had not existed before.

Elmira had previously been a whiskey-only drinking town, and good at it. Now lager beer was being drunk by the barrel. This really riled the old Temperance portion of locals.

In the 1850s, Elmira had three breweries all owned by German immigrants. The Hockenburger brewery stood on the site of today's Shulman's scrap yard – stumbling distance to the steel rolling mills and the canal. With the breweries came saloons – near the railroad depot and near the military barracks at Madison and East Washington Avenues. When Elmira became a city in 1864, one could visit any of its sixty saloons.

In the 1830s, Elmira already had established the Chemung Canal, the Junction Canal, Baldwin Street Academy, predecessor of the Elmira Free Academy for serious students, and Second Street Cemetery. Well-laid out streets were an advantage to the village.

In the 1840s, Elmira had a telegraph office, a fire department, several newspapers, and the Plank Road (Pennsylvania Avenue to the Penn-

Photograph of early Lake Street looking north from Water Street in Elmira by photographer W. J. Moulton in 1854. Courtesy of the Eleanor Barnes Library.

sylvania state line). Peter Biggs ran a soap factory at the corner of East Fifth and Madison Avenue. John W. Jones served as the sexton of the First Baptist Church, and secretly worked hard helping escaped Southern slaves find their way in the North. Jones was not yet known for what he would be doing for Confederate prisoners at the Elmira Prison camp twenty years hence.

By the 1850s, Elmira already had a YMCA, Woodlawn Cemetery, The Elmira Female College, Seeley Absalom's soda pop factory on the south side of the river, music teachers, and a school board. Elmira also had twenty doctors including African-Americans and women.

The Eric Railroad had joined Elmira in 1849 by connecting to the rail lines of New York, Boston, Washington DC, Buffalo, Rochester, and Chicago. Elmira's location made it a hub for service in all directions. Hotels and restaurants boomed on Wisner Street (the name eventually changed to Railroad Avenue). Beautiful hotels provided the luxuries and amenities of the mid-nineteenth-century. Elmira entertained its greatest group of politicos one night in 1851, when Stephen A. Douglas and William H. Seward checked in to the Rathbun Hotel. President Millard Fillmore and his Secretary of State, Daniel Webster, registered across the street at the Mansion House. They were celebrating the completion of the Erie Railroad. President Fillmore spoke from the Mansion House and Stephen Douglas from the Rathbun's balcony.

Rumblings about Elmira becoming a city started in the newspapers around 1857. Some advantages to incorporating as a city were the ability to raise taxes and provide better services like having a paid fire department, better police protection, control of property assessments, holding its own elections, and the ability to organize its own government.

In 1864, Elmira became a city with 13,000 inhabitants. At the time, it was served by two railroads the Erie and the Northern Central. The Chemung Canal was still in use. Wisner Street offered many small hotels like the American, the Delevan, the Eagle, and Hoffman's. Briggs Brewery stood at the corner of East Second and today's Clemens Center Parkway. The Partridge Planing mill occupied the land where the Steele Memorial Library stands today. Many old dilapidated shacks and lumberyards were near the Canal. The brand new Andrews and Burbage Saw Factory was on the northwest corner of East Church Street and the canal. On the southwest corner was Congdon's malt house at about the location of to-day's Clemens Performing Arts Center. Looking far north up the Canal from this site one could see a group of shed-like buildings with many iron smoke stacks and the glow of the open furnaces of the Steel Rolling Mills near Washington Avenue.

On Baldwin Street stood the Pattinson House at the corner of East Water. Vaudevillians performed at Ely's Hall on the northeast corner of Carroll and Baldwin.

By 1864, Elmira had already met Jervis Langdon, although not yet as Samuel Clemens' father-in-law. Langdon was well known in Elmira's high circles. He owned many logging and coal mining organizations that profited his bank accounts.

Thomas K. Beecher was the pastor of Elmira's Independent Congregational church. He was easily Elmira's most provocative character. He came from an illustrious, sometimes notorious family. More conservative, Beecher held an anti-abolition stance even though he had some participation in the local Underground Railroad.

Elmira was now an incorporated city. John Arnot was a banker; his son John, Jr. was Elmira's first mayor. The Pratt brothers Daniel and Ransom ran the Woolen Mills on East Avenue. The Pratt Factory had a government contract for 1,600 yards of cloth daily. The Rolling Mills were paying high wages for the hot and sweaty work of manufacturing steel rail. The mills ran day and night with more than 400 employees and a monthly payroll of $47,000.

In the photograph on page 34, you see a wonderful photograph of old downtown Elmira - Lake Street looking north, circa 1854, attributed to W. J. Moulton. Moulton was a photographer in Elmira in the middle and latter 1800s. It is fascinating to note that within the streets and buildings visible in his photo – there were actually 137 businesses located in this two-block area. Among them were: five shoe stores, eight groceries, three barber shops, two photographers, two hotels, a bowling alley, the main post office, two boarding houses, two bakeries, two butchers, four billiard parlors, a blacksmith, a hat shop, two doctors' offices, two newspapers, five law offices, a livery stable, three tailors, two printers, two saloons, a bookstore, a music school, two restaurants, a furniture store, a fruit market, a hardware store, a tobacco store, a lumber store, a candy store, an ax manufacturer, and a wig maker.

I found some interesting names and businesses on Lake Street from the 1863 Elmira directory. Note that the addresses are the "old" numbering system.

The Arbour Hotel, Saloon, and Billiards were located at numbers 7, 9, and 11 Lake Street. The Arnot residence (now the Arnot Art Museum) was number 57 Lake Street. Christopher Atkins ran his tailor shop at the corner of Lake and Water Streets. John Baker, Sr. was the Lake Street bridge toll-keeper, because you could not get between the north and south sides without paying a toll. The Lake Street Bridge was a continuation of the Plank Road – the toll road to the Pennsylvania state line. You could sit for your photograph at Abraham Hart's studio at 22 Lake Street.

Haight's Hotel was on the southwest corner of Lake and Cross, today's Market Street. Owen McGreevy ran a livery stable next to the hotel for the travelling patrons. Dr. William F. Goodman (colored) practiced medicine at 52 Lake Street. James B. Culp served refreshments at his saloon at 44 Lake Street. Levi Coke was a baker, confectioner and grocer at 31 Lake Street. Gabriel Barr kept an "intelligence office" at 56 Lake Street.

George Beebe practiced law at 4 Lake Street. At 39 Lake Street was the Hitchcock and Loomis butcher shop. Maurice Levy sold tobacco at 33 Lake Street. Abraham Krowl shoed horses at his a blacksmith shop at 38 Lake Street. McKinney & Swan sold insurance at 2 Lake Street. Lewis Mackol was a shoemaker inside Haight's Hotel. Richard Morris ran a grocery at 5 Lake Street. B.P Beardsley manufactured axes at his factory at 50 Lake Street.

In 2014, people say Elmira has changed, that it is not like it "used to be." Does anything remain of that old Elmira? Yes, some architecture from early days – the Arnot Art Museum, the Chemung County courthouse complex, the Chemung County Historical Society, wonderful old houses in the Near Westside, business buildings in the Lake and Carroll

The edge of this albumin photograph says, "Panoramic View of Elmira from Hose Tower - looking North West." Image courtesy of Diane Janowski.

area, and the Erie railroad depot. One can still see traces of the Chemung Canal near Eldridge Park. One rolling mill building is still in use by F. M. Howell & Co.

Some street names mark important landmarks - Canal Street, Railroad Avenue, College Avenue, Academy Place. Others are named for community leaders – Hoffman, Gray, Church, William, Fox, Baldwin, LaFrance, Sly, and Carroll. Place and building names honor our local people and events – Brand Park, Arnot Art Museum, Chemung Canal Trust, Wisner Park, Steele Memorial Library, Arnot Health, and John W. Jones Museum. Elmira has physically changed, and while we do not always remember the significance of places and things, our legacy is all around us.

Bibliography:

"Beecher Family." Harriet Beecher Stowe Center. Harriet Beecher Stowe Center, n.d. Web. 3 Dec. 2014. <https://www.harrietbeecherstowecenter.org/hbs/beecher_family.shtml>.

Booth, Arthur. "Fantasy Pictures the Growing Elmira of 75 years Ago." *Star-Gazette* [Elmira, NY] 27 June 1939, morning ed.: 6A. Print.

Brigham, A. DeLancey, comp. *Elmira Directory*. Elmira, NY: Hall Brothers, 1857-1863. Print.

Horrigan, Michael. "Antebellum Elmira." *Chemung Historical Journal* 48.1 (September 2002): 5249-5260. Print.

Janowski, Diane. *ChemungHistory.com's Big Book of Pictures*. Elmira, NY: New York History Review, 2009.

Towner, Ausburn. *Our County and Its People, A History of the County and Valley of Chemung from the closing years of the eighteenth century*.: D. Mason & Co., 1892

Fire Engine Capital

by James Hare

The village of Elmira was incorporated in 1828. That same year three fire wardens were selected. Over time, volunteer companies formed and were disbanded and new ones started. Competition among the organizations could be fierce. Sometimes, when more than one company responded to a fire, there was a race for the water supply, and in the scramble fistfights often broke out and volunteers might step on each other's hoses. Often the house burnt down.

Upon becoming a city in 1864, the competition was between Republicans and Democrats, in the famous "fire engine fight" shortly after incorporation. Up to that time Elmira fires were fought with a couple of old fashioned hand-fed fire engines. According to a 1921 Elmira *Telegram* article, "when it came to purchasing our first steam fire engine there were two active contestants for the honor—and Elmira's money. One was an Amoskeag made somewhere down-east and the other a Sillsbee, manufactured in Seneca Falls." Apparently the final test took place on the Main Street bridge with a committee led by Democratic Alderman De Bruce Goodell, an Amoskeag adherent, and Republican Alderman Charles G. Fairman, a Sillsbee supporter conducting the contest. "At times the fight was quite furious. Our worthy city officials confined themselves to an abbreviated alphabet, but the boys sometimes resorted to ever ready youthful fists upon the least provocation." After weeks of wrangling they decided to buy both, one a rotary and the other a piston engine.

It only seems logical that from this beginning Elmira would become the "Fire Engine Capital of the World."

While the Common Council argued over which steam engine to purchase, a young man named Truckson LaFrance came to Elmira. A descendant of a family of French Huguenots, he was born in Susquehanna County, Pennsylvania on September 14, 1834. Truckson was the oldest of five sons born to Willis and Clarissa LaFrance. He had an "inventive mind" and came to Elmira seeking employment.

AMERICAN-LA FRANCE FIRE ENGINE CO., ELMIRA. N. Y.

Postcard view published by Rubin Brothers, Elmira. Courtesy of the Eleanor Barnes Library.

A. Ward LaFrance, nephew of Truckson, wrote that the *Daily Advertiser* purchased the first power press in the city introducing it at an open house. But on that day it did not work. "A modest young man suggested a remedy" when no one else could solve the problem. "What do you know about a press? He was asked. Nothing was the answer, but I think if you will do as I suggest, she will be alright." He fixed it and was hired by the *Advertiser*. He also became an "engineer" for the fire department.

Truckson would eventually obtain a job at the Elmira Union Iron Works where in the early 1870's he was able to secure several patents on improvements he developed in the rotary steam engine. The basic improvement he patented was the "nest tube boiler" which strengthened the most unreliable part of the early engines. John Vischer, head of the Iron Works, became interested and was convinced by Truckson to manufacture a steam fire engine. A short time later they had a small fire engine business going.

"Their efforts attracted the attention of some wealthy local men and they bought out the operation on April 17, 1873 founding the LaFrance Manufacturing Company. Vischer became a director and Truckson LaFrance was employed as an engineer. The principal founder-owners were General Alexander S. Diven and his four sons, who were prominent lawyers and civic leaders." By July of 1873, they had purchased about ten acres and constructed a small plant on the old "Keg Factory" grounds in Southport, producing the first steam engine by the end of the year.

Truckson was the quiet inventive brother. In 1876, his younger brother Asa joined the company. He was the "quick thinking, hard driving man in the field." When the Civil War ended, the one armed Asa, a "born musician" as well as a mechanic, was a member of the New York Veterans Cavalry Band. After his enlistment he spent a number of years on the professional stage, appearing with the Cal Wagner Minstrels. He was known as a fine cornetist and took part in many concerts as a soloist. In 1868, he organized a sixteen member band in Elmira. He was described as "the liveliest little brass band boy of his day." He was ten years younger than Truckson.

In the early days, selling fire engines was very competitive. The brothers had to resort to ingenuity at times to make a sale. Because a salesman had promised a little too much to the Bridgeport, Connecticut Department, the officials added a little extra touch to make the test more difficult. "To eliminate the possibility of a spurt test, they placed the engine behind a building out of sight of the open tank into which water was to be discharged to measure the actual gallons per minute pumping capacity of the engine. Asa placed his twelve-year-old son on a shed in sight of both engine and tank. When the nozzles were directed into the tank, the young "stranger" was told to wave a handkerchief as a signal. So the canny demonstrator was enabled to conserve his boiler pressure until the precise moment when it was most needed." Asa made the sale and the Bridgeport firemen never knew their "out of sight" test was not as accurate as they had planned.

The Company began to manufacture other fire fighting equipment and in 1880 became the LaFrance Fire Engine Company. The 1890s was an era of business consolidation with the growth of trusts. A rival firm was created named the American Fire Engine Company. With the idea of creating a monopoly, in 1900 the International Fire Engine Company was announced. It included the American Fire Engine Company, LaFrance Fire Engine Company, and Thomas Manning Jr. and Company. Three support equipment manufacturers were included, three fire extinguisher manufacturers also joined the company. In 1903, the company reorganized into the American LaFrance Fire Engine Company, and in 1906 company headquarters were relocated from New York City to Elmira.

In 1959, it was estimated that 50,000 pieces of fire apparatus were in active service in the United States and Canada, with 30,000 of those designed by American LaFrance. Truckson LaFrance died in 1895 at the age of 61. Asa, who would establish a "wonderfully successful automobile business" died in 1927 at the age of 82.

In January 2014 American LaFrance went out of business for the third time. The company closed its "ancestral plant" in Elmira in 1985. It reappeared the following year, "a much smaller entity" in Bluefield, Virginia.

Eight years later that firm shutdown. In 1996, Freightliner Corporation revived ALF, and in 2001 the firm relocated to Charleston, South Carolina. In 2008, it moved to a plant in Summerville, South Carolina. Apparently a fourth new plant was opened in 2013 but its last owner, Patriach Partners has "pulled the plug."

Stereoview of Gleasons' Water Cure facility by Charles Tomlinson circa 1880. Albumin photograph courtesy of Eleanor Barnes Library.

Gleasons' Water Cure

by Diane Janowski

Modern hydropathy – a system of treating illnesses using water was developed in Austria in the 1820s. By the 1840s, there were several "water cure" health resorts in Europe. Treatments included cold-water therapy, walking, and eating simple peasant food. Doctors wrapped cold wet sheets around wealthy European patients for several hours to cure them of their ailments.

Drs. Silas and Rachel Gleason opened Gleason's Water Cure on East Hill on June 1, 1852. The main building had four stories with two wings. A smaller building was two stories. The facility accommodated 100 patients at a time. According to the 1863 city directory, "The beautiful natural surroundings made it a desirable location for the invalid." Their advertisement also mentioned that patients were to bring their own towels (a minimum of six would be needed).

The natural sulphur spring resort brought a new theory of healthcare to the United States. The strong-smelling water was pumped into the buildings with wooden pipes. The Gleasons practiced hydropathic medicine using water as a cure and a preventative. It not only used water as a therapeutic agent, but the facility also promoted temperance and women's rights. Silas Gleason studied traditional medicine at Castleton Medical College and graduated in 1844. Rachel Gleason was one of the first women to receive a medical diploma in the United States.

Hydrotherapy was "gentle" as opposed to the more invasive medical treatments of the time. The Gleasons prescribed hot and cold-water baths, water sprays, electrical immersions in water to their patients. Hygiene, good eating, exercise, abstention from coffee, alcohol, and smoking rounded out the Gleason treatment. In addition, an "aggressive course of water drinking" was expected.

Gleasons' patients wore "Bloomer costumes" – gowns with very wide sleeves and puffy loose-fitting pants. Rachel Gleason believed that tight women's clothing caused most health problems. Women patients usually cut their hair short so it would dry quicker from the frequent baths. In her *Letters to The People on Health and Happiness*, Rachel described her treatment as "simple diet, pure air, hard beds, proper positions by night and day, and a regular, systematic training to invigorate the whole of the muscular system by appropriate exercise combined with the medical use of water as a tonic to the whole nervous and muscular system. In most cases, this would restore 'perfect health.'"

The Gleasons were also able to spend more time with their patients as they were with them all day. The Gleasons believed that women physicians bonded better with women patients. Women patients also recuperated better in a female environment.

Rachel's specialty was the diseases of women. She was Olivia Langdon Clemens's physician and delivered all four Clemens children. Among Mrs. Gleason's patients were Elizabeth Cady Stanton, Susan B. Anthony, and Emily Dickinson's mother. All came to Elmira for treatments. Elmira was world-famous, and highly acclaimed for its hospital.

The Water Cure was also moderately expensive making it appealing to higher-class families. In the 1860s, the Gleasons charged $7–10 a week for live-in treatments. The Gleasons were there until 1868 when Silas's health forced them to move to Florida.

After the Gleasons retired, other doctors followed in succession including Dr. Theron Augustus Wales and his wife Zippie Wales from 1873-1897, Dr. Edith Wheeler, Dr. Clarabelle Hutchinson, Dr. Fannie Brown, and finally in 1927, Drs. John and Gertrude Doyle. Attending staff was predominantly female as were the clientele.

The Water Cure lasted until 1902, although the building was used as a rest home until 1959.

The "Cures" at Elmira and nearby Dansville, New York, were headed by strong staffs and succeeded for many decades unlike four other cures in Massachusetts that failed.

Sources:

Wash and Be Healed: The Water-Cure Movement and Women's Health. Susan Cayleff page 92.

The Routledge Encyclopedia of Mark Twain, edited by J.R. LeMaster, James D. Wilson page 322.

http://www.sciencemuseum.org.uk/broughttolife/techniques/hydropathy.aspx

Mark Twain and Medicine: Any Mummery Will Cure. K. Patrick Ober.

Communication from Mrs. Dr. R. B. Gleason, in Catharine E. Beecher, Letters to The People on Health and Happiness (New York: Harper & Brothers, 1856), pp. 1*-16*

Iszard's and the New Downtown

by James Hare

Headquarters for ***Wall Paper***	# S. F. IZARD CO. Corner Water and Baldwin Streets	SPECIAL SALE of **Men's Soft SHIRTS** 75c Value at....... **50c**

Advertisement in the Elmira *Daily Gazette & Free Press* May 25, 1904.

Fans of PBS's Masterpiece Theatre are currently watching Mr. Selfridge. Harry Gordon Selfridge was a protégée of retail magnate Marshal Field of Chicago. Selfridge was a marketing genius who introduced American retail methods to London in 1909. Five years earlier, in 1904, Samuel French Iszard opened his "department store" in Elmira. Iszard was also a protégée, but of John Wanamaker of Philadelphia, another merchandise advertising genius who popularized the fixed price system and created the money- back guarantee.

Elmira boomed during and after the Civil War. In 1886, a pamphlet proclaimed that "there is not an inland city in the east that can compete with Elmira..." Indeed there were 21 hotels in the city during the 1880's. Elmira's Water Street was the "first shopping center", with much of the activity east of Baldwin Street. Historian Tom Byrne noted that "the retail and wholesale trade help establish Elmira as the "Queen City" in the late 19th and early 20th centuries."

S. F. Iszard (1868-1949) began his career as a stock boy for a clothier in Philadelphia. By age 19, he wanted to go into the wholesale business as a "salesman or drummer..." Eventually he held a responsible position in the Wanamaker organization and it was reported he had a "close friendship" with him. Iszard, while on the road, established a relationship with Dey Brothers, a dry goods store, in Elmira. In 1904, he purchased their business on the corner of Baldwin and Water Streets.

From 1904-1922, the Iszard store showed such steady growth that a newer and larger facility was needed. The company investigated various sites looking for one that would allow a new building to be constructed. In a bold move the Iszard Company purchased "one of the most desirable" properties in the city on Main Street for $75,000. Ground was broken on November 23, 1922. Local architects Pierce and Bickford (who had designed City Hall) were hired to put together what the newspaper described as the perfect store plan. According to the paper it would be "one of the most modern department stores in this section of the country", it went on to report that an "exclusive feature... will be a soda fountain and ice cream parlor" which was not designed for profit but as an "attractive feature of service... perfect service was to be the keynote of every detail of the new up-to-the minute department store." Of course for all those who still remember shopping at Iszard's, the Tea Room was a feature when the store opened in November of 1924.

The decision by Iszard's to move west and build a new four story building on Main Street shifted the center of gravity for Elmira's downtown. The December 6, 1926 Elmira *Star-Gazette* headline "Elaborate Business Block To Be Erected at Location Leased by Clothing Company" announced the decision of the owners of Gorton Company (one of Elmira's leading women's and children's wearing apparel concerns) to acquire the corner of Main and Water Streets with plans to build a new four story building. News reports said the unpublished price involved in the 51-year lease was the "greatest in money value, of any lease ever written in the city."

Within three years of the Gorton lease the new one million dollar, eight story Mark Twain Hotel opened on the north side of Iszard's in 1929. It became the "Queen of the Queen City." S. F. Iszard noted that, "as a whole the Mark Twain is most fascinating to me. I have traveled extensively abroad and throughout the United States and I have not seen anything in a community of this size to equal it. It is a splendid improvement to Elmira." The *Star-Gazette* offered another citizen's observation, "I can't believe that I'm in Elmira, it seems so metropolitan."

Iszard's logo from 1978.

Iszard's logo from 1986.

Things you don't know about Iszard's

By Diane Janowski

Those of us past a certain age remember our beloved Iszards on North Main Street. We recollect the brown bread they served in the Tea Room, and visiting with Santa after the big Christmas Parade. We remember the flagpole, the clock, and the overhanging awning. We loved riding in the elevator with the criss-cross gate and the uniformed attendant. And, we can still see the money going up through that skinny chute.

But, there are some things about Iszards that you may not know.

At the age of nineteen, Samuel French Iszard of Philadelphia went on the road as a salesman for Strawbridge & Clothier. One of his frequent stops was the Dey Brothers department store (soon after known as Reynold's Big Store) on the corner of East Water and Baldwin Streets (still there). Iszard bought this store in 1904. He, and his family moved here from Germantown, Pennsylvania.

Iszard opened his new building in November 1924 at 150 North Main Street. Within six years, the Mark Twain Hotel opened next door. It was great as the hotel brought a steady stream of out of-town travelers to shop at Elmira's biggest department store.

Back in 1939, Iszards advertised that it was "air cooled" from sixty feet under the sidewalk on North Main Street. Apparently "under Iszards is a large quantity of water on a bed of round, smooth rocks." They guessed it was an underground spring, as the water temperature was measured at a steady 52°. No matter what time of year the temperature was always 52°.

So how did Iszards use that cold water for air conditioning? The advertisement claimed, "A large pump draws over 200 gallons-per-minute from sixty-feet down. This water is pumped through radiators in the build-ing. Fresh air is blown over these radiators by a powerful four-foot fan to different parts of the store."

The air cooled as it passed over the radiators. A dehumidifier re-moved the excess moisture. Iszards claimed that "as the air is recirculated, it passes through spun glass filters and most of the dust which is injurious to health is removed."

Because Iszards had so many customers in the store at one time, they breathed up much of the good oxygen. For this reason, an electric ozonifier added oxygen to the air in the store. "As a result our store is a healthy, as well as a comfortable place to shop."

Miss America 1926 was Norma Smallwood of Bristow, Oklahoma. Norma won both the bathing suit and evening gown contests in the pageant. Instead of returning to school after her win, she instead chose to tour the US with her mother, on the Orpheum Circuit for $1,500 a week. One of her stops was Iszards. On July 22, 1927, nineteen-year-old Norma sat on view in Iszards front corner window wearing the swimming outfit that won her the title at Atlantic City. After the window sitting, she put on a small fashion show modeling all of Iszard's finest women's clothing. Later in that day she sang and danced for a large audience at the Grotto Club (now Joy Crest). Elmira was lucky to see her – she stopped showing up to her scheduled appearances a few weeks later when she claimed the circuit paid her only half of her expected salary. Norma returned to Atlantic City in September 1927 but did not retain her title.

Iszard's was a four-generation store with branches in the Arnot Mall and on the Commons in Ithaca. Iszard's closed its Elmira stores in 1988.

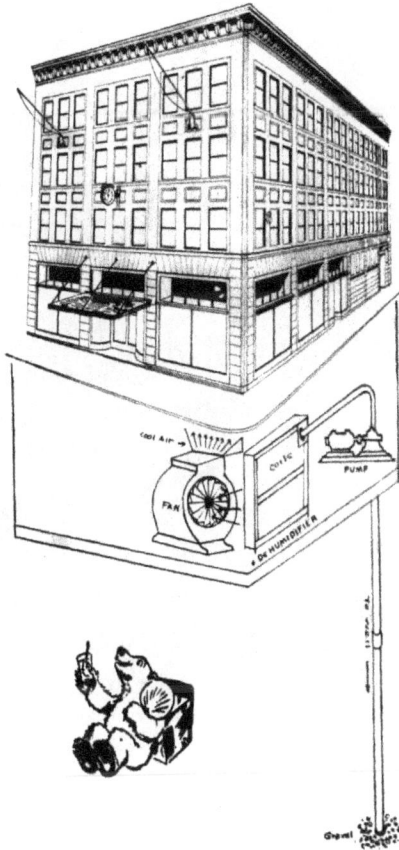

Iszard's cooling system. From the Elmira *Star-Gazette* June 27, 1939 edition.

Esther Baker Steele 1835 - 1911
In 1899 she gave Elmira a wonderful gift
- a free public library in the name
of her late husband Joel Dorman Steele.

Second Steele Memorial Library

by James Hare

"*T*he Steele Memorial Library hardly knew itself in a new home. But the books, which for so many years had stood side by side in the Steele Memorial building gave it a familiar air, and they, like the library staff, were happy in having room enough so they were not jostled about by their neighbors and had space for new friends," so observed Mrs. Kate Deane Andrew, head librarian, to the Steele Memorial Library board of trustees on February 16, 1924. The second Steele Memorial Library had opened a year earlier on February 8, 1923. She went on to note that, "the beautiful new Carnegie building, which is spacious and convenient gives a feeling of freedom to all who enter."

The need for a "new" library building had been apparent for some time.

In the autumn of 1915, Henry D. Whitfield of New York stopped off in Elmira to spend the night with his Harvard classmate, Philip D. Sawyer. Sawyer was a trustee of the library and his office was in the same building. Mr. Whitfield was interested in the "character" of the building and asked to see the library. Noting the "cramped" quarters on the fourth and fifth floor, he said, "Why don't you get a Carnegie library, I will help you." No small commitment as his sister was Mrs. Andrew Carnegie.

This was not the first offer of a Carnegie Library to Elmira. It seems that at the time of the opening of the first library (1899) discussion of a Carnegie grant of $100,000 had been underway. In 1922, the Elmira *Star-Gazette* commented that, "it is quite certain that the Elmira politicians who then decried and prevented a Carnegie Library when it was offered were sadly and grievously in the wrong. Elmira has long suffered from such politicians." One reason for turning aside the grant was the requirement that the city commit to an annual expenditure of 10% of the grant on maintenance of the library. Binghamton received a $75,000 grant in 1902.

Years later Mrs. Andrew offered another reason for a new library. She noted that, "especially annoying to the patrons was the undependable elevator leading to the stacks. It consistently gave out and people would come puffing up the stairs red-faced from the unexpected exertion. I was in constant fear of apoplectic patients." (Author note: the elevator at the present library has just been repaired.)

Within a year of Mr. Whitfield's visit Elmira was poised to accept a Carnegie grant. On January 29, 1916 it was reported that the Carnegie Corporation of New York had "voted a fund of $70,000 to the City of Elmira with which to erect a Carnegie Library in the city." It was the greatest single gift to the city up to that time. The city would agree to provide an "approved" site and $7,000 per year for maintenance. The library trustees would mortgage their building for an amount ($25,000) sufficient to buy a new site. The library would relocate to the new building and rental income from the old building would pay taxes, insurance, repairs and eventually pay off the mortgage.

BUT, there were complications. When the YMCA and the Steele Memorial Library Association had agreed to build the first library there was a stipulation that if the building ceased being a library, ownership reverted back to the YMCA, which had provided the land. This potentially "fatal" clause was eliminated when the Y agreed to "waive all of their rights under an existing agreement to any interest in the Steele Memorial Library." In addition, the Elmira situation was unique in that the city was not asked to furnish the site, it was provided by the Steele Memorial Library Association.

Five sites were considered. The corner of Church and State Streets was rejected by Mr. Whitfield. The southeast corner of Main and Gray Streets was attractive because of the parks. The lot on the west side of Lake Street, just south of the Arnot Art Gallery had appeal. Architect Whitfield thought ideal was the two acres of ground of the Arnot Homestead at the northwest corner of Clinton Street and Park Place because of its closeness to the college.

The site selected was the "palatial" Reynolds mansion on the southeast corner of Church and Lake Streets. (Mrs. Reynolds was the daughter of Dr. Edwin Eldridge). The purchase price was $22,000, with the Library

Steele Memorial Library, Elmira, N. Y.

18204

The second Steele Memorial Library now the Chemung County Chamber of Commerce building on East Church Street. Postcard view published by Queen City Paper Company, Elmira.

Association contributing $20,000 and the city $2,000. An editorial comment read, "citizens who take a broad view of things regard the place as on the wrong side of the city. Such citizens also stop to reflect that some day, not far off, the city and county should own the entire block bounded by Market, Lake, Church and William Streets to be used wholly for public buildings."

With plans complete and a new library building to be erected "without delay," the United States entered World War I. All major construction projects were placed on hold and the Carnegie Corporation agreed to defer the grant.

When the war ended, a $70,000 building in 1916, cost $140-150,000 in 1920. In August of 1920, Mayor George W. Peck led a delegation to New York City to see if the appropriation could be increased. The Carnegie Corporation awarded an additional $40,000 (bringing their total to $110,000) provided the city make an additional appropriation of $40,000 to be spent before receiving their grant. The city was willing to agree but a controversy erupted over control of the library board of trustees. Alderman Cornelius O'Dea argued that, "if Elmira is to have a public library then it should be a public library in every sense of the word." The key phrase was "the establishment" of a public library which placed it under New York State education law requiring control by the Mayor and Council.

Eventually, a compromise resulted in a ten member board with five public members and five library association members who self recruited.

On Monday, August 22, 1921, with "appropriate ceremony," the cornerstone was laid. John M. Connally, chair of the building committee, stated, "let us hope that the cornerstone so carefully laid will not only be a cornerstone of a great library, but that it will also be the cornerstone for a better a more cultured Elmira."

Eventually one question would remain. What will be the library's name?

There was a general desire in the city to perpetuate the name of Mrs. Esther Baker Steele, however the city was "deeply grateful" to the Andrew Carnegie Corporation. Mrs. Andrew noted the library could be called by any name, "so long as appreciation of its gift is realized."

Achievement Club boosts confidence for many Elmirans

By Diane Janowski

The name Rufus Stanley doesn't ring as many bells as it used to, but he was a very important local person back in the 1920s. When he first arrived in Elmira in 1885, he worked with the YMCA. Later that year he started the Rambling Club to "promote the welfare of young men of Elmira." Members of the club "tramped and camped, winter and summer." It was a way for young men to disperse their extra energy. Within a few years many members carried Kodak's new invention – the personal camera - on their outings.

In 1898, Rufus started the Handicraft Club. In 1901came his Rural School Club to teach boys and girls gardening and cooking. The Omega Club taught Elmira children the same skills. In 1907, Rufus started the Corn Club, that in 1909 was renamed the Chemung County Agricultural Club. The Poultry Club and the Bread Making Club were added in 1910. Rufus also began taking members of his clubs to Albany and Washington, DC. Rufus did a lot of work through the College of Agriculture at Cornell University and the Geneva Experiment Station.

In 1914, with federal funding that created Cornell Cooperative Extension, Rufus was given more responsibility. With sanctioning under the federal government, he renamed his whole operation the Achievement Club. It then included "potato growing, canning, sewing, home yard development, poultry, pig, calf, and rabbit raising." During the quiet cold winters "the boys built potato crates and were instructed in the simple use of work tools."

In 1919, Rufus became Chemung County's first 4-H club agent. His work eventually pioneered activities adopted by national 4-H clubs.

The Knier family, parents Charles and Pearl with their eleven children, knew how to be resourceful. In 1922, sister Dorothy entered the Chemung County Fair with her exhibit of canned goods that were enough for one person to live on for an entire year. In 1923, she won the Achievement Club's honor of going to Washington during Easter week. Dorothy had been a member of the club for four years. Her specialty was canning vegetables. Between 1920 and 1923, she "put up" 1,495 cans of produce worth nearly $3,000. The vegetables were raised by her brothers in the family garden at 1002 College Avenue.

In 1924, Dorothy's twin brothers John and Charles won the club's contest. They had used two vacant city lots for growing vegetables, and built their own greenhouses. In their greenhouses they successfully grew peanuts. They worked every day after attending Elmira Free Academy. They built their own irrigation system for dry times. In their four years in the Achievement Club they raised vegetables worth $1,400 with a seed investment of $56.40. They sold their produce every Tuesday and Saturday at the City Market.

During Easter week 1924, the champions went by train first to the coalmines at Scranton, then a whole day in Philadelphia, before arriving in Washington, DC. The visitors saw the Washington Monument, Lincoln Memorial, Mount Vernon, and the White House. The high point of the club's trip was meeting President Coolidge.

Two years later Rufus Stanley died while talking to a reunion of former Rambling Club members. In his years of service, Rufus helped many of the boys and girls to become outstanding members of our community.

Sources:

Elmira *Star-Gazette* March 31, 1923 page 3
Elmira *Star-Gazette* April 17, 1924 page 7
Elmira Star-Gazette July 9, 1926 page 1
Elmira *Star-Gazette* April 22, 1924 page 4
Brooklyn *Daily Eagle* May 18, 1924 page 96

http://www.waymarking.com/waymarks/WMR6H9_Rufus_Stanley_Monument_Bas_Relief_Harris_Hill_Park_Top_of_Harris_Hill_Big_Flats_NY
http://chemung.cce.cornell.edu/4-h-youth/our-history

John and Charles Knier, 14 year old twin brothers, raised vegetables valued at $500 on a city lot in Elmira, NY. For their achievement, they won
a trip to Washington, DC from the Department of Agriculture. Harris
and Ewing, photographers. Courtesy of Library of Congress Prints and
Photographs Division.

Frederick Douglass Connects with Elmira

by James Hare

"His appearance was loudly cheered, and this true lover of his race delivered one of the strongest addresses ever heard in Elmira. As the venerated and noble colored man (sic) stood on the platform, with his head bared, his white and heavy locks, his massive frame and kindly eyes gave him the appearance of a Moses of his race..." and "the foremost colored man (sic) in the world...." So wrote the Elmira *Daily Advertiser* on August 4, 1880. The newspaper was reporting on the huge event which took place the day before as the "Colored People" of Elmira celebrated the anniversary of Britain's liberation of slaves (1834)

Frederick Douglass, circa 1879. Photograph by G.K. Warren. Courtesy of National Archives and Records Administration.

and the Emancipation Proclamation (1863) merged into a day of song, a parade, and speeches.

There were delegations present from "almost every considerable place within one hundred miles of Elmira." The festivities even reached "the white folks" as the streets were "thronged with expectant people." The speeches and ceremonies at Hoffman Grove were preceded by a grand parade formed at Temperance Hall on Baldwin Street. The LaFrance Band, in their new uniforms ("dark blue and the neatest we have ever seen") followed the Grand Marshal and preceded a host of contingents from Syracuse, Geneva, Horseheads, Corning and many others. John W. Jones was "President of the Day." According to the paper, "a sumptuous dinner will be

served on the grounds of the Union and Zion churches. Arrangements are made to make this the grandest celebration ever held in the State." The festivities would close with a grand ball at Military Hall. Supper at the Wyckoff House including a ball ticket would cost $2.

Douglass spoke at Hoffman Grove. Being an election year, he addressed the campaign. He gave a "calm, dispassionate and truthful history of the two great political parties... and shows beyond all doubt or question which is the party of freedom and progress and which is the party of oppression and intolerance." Douglass supported Republican James A. Garfield for President.

Frederick Douglass had a deep and heartfelt connection to Elmira. In 1838, during his escape from slavery, he was taken in by Jervis Langdon and his wife at their home in Millport. Thirty years later he told Jervis' widow, "when it was an invitation to the incendiary, your husband took me home sick, nursed, cared for and treated me as a Mother and now it is his son who invites me in days when hospitality yet costs something to give."

Over the years, Douglass visited Elmira many times. In February 1872, he lectured at the Opera House on "the wrongs which his race had suffered in Santo Domingo before the chains of slavery were broken there." The *Daily Advertiser* called it, "the best lecture of the season." During this visit he stayed one night at the Langdon home prior to his lecture but was to leave at 4 AM the next morning on the train. Not wanting to disturb the family he planned to stay at a hotel. He asked Charles Langdon to go with him and as Charles was bidding him good bye and about to drive off, "Frederick put his hand on his arm and said, "Will you please come in with me? 'Of course,' said Charles. I went and found that if I hadn't, the wretched little rat who keeps the hotel would have said no to him. Fortunately he is in my debt and had to mind his P's and Q's." (this event was reported by Anna Dickinson in a letter to a friend.)

Douglass returned to Elmira in 1873 to celebrate the passage of Civil Rights Amendments and legislation. Like the event in 1880, there was a parade to Hoffman Grove and much celebration. The "President of the Day" was John W. Jones. The parade was led by a detachment of Elmira police followed by the LaFrance's Cornet Band. After the speeches, the procession reformed and returned to Dickinson Street. Douglass spoke that evening at the Opera House. According to the newspaper, he "impressed upon his hearers... that now the rights of colored man had been given him in their full measure, he should take every means to demonstrate himself worthy of them." The paper called it one of Mr. Douglass' "finest efforts."

Elmira's first African-American Church began in 1841. In 1848 it was named the African Methodist Episcopal Zion Church. It was located at Dickinson and Fourth Streets. Calvin Brewer wrote in the *Chemung Historical Journal*, "for many years the African Methodist Episcopal Zion Church would remain a popular attraction for conferences, district functions, Christian socials, and other religious events for the community without regard to ethnicity. The Church was rededicated in 1894 as the Frederick Douglass African Methodist Episcopal Zion Church. In 1895, at Douglass' death, "Memorial" was officially added to the name of the church commemorating the renowned abolitionist. The church would now and forever be known as the "Frederick Douglass Memorial African Methodist Episcopal Zion Church of Elmira, New York."

The original building, "the towering edifice" was demolished in 1951 to make way for Jones Court. A second building was erected at 414 Baldwin Street but was vacated in 1995 when the church merged with the Minnie L. Floyd AME Zion Church at Madison Avenue and Second Street. Calvin Brewer noted, "the quest for a hallowed place where freed men can work, thrive and be revived remains steadfast as the spirit of Frederick Douglass Memorial African Methodist Episcopal Zion Church moves ever forward in the future."

John Hendy, An Early Settler of Elmira

By Diane Janowski

Postcard view of John Hendy's cabin. Publisher unknown. Courtesy of the Eleanor Barnes Library.

E lmira is 150 years old in 2014. But, isn't Elmira older than that?

Cartographer Guy Johnson drew the first map of our area in 1771, called "Country of the Six Nations." Chemung County was still a blank space. General John Sullivan destroyed the Indian village of Kanaweola (near today's Kennedy Valve) in 1779. Four years later in 1783, Matthias Hollenback opened the first local trading post near today's Holiday Inn on East Water Street. A few settlers arrived after the 1786 Treaty of Fort Stanwix that, theoretically, made our region safe for white settlers. The

Iroquois were to remain in western New York. The villages of Newtown, Wisnerburg, and Dewittsburg combined into "Village of Newtown" in 1790. The name changed from "Village of Newtown" to "Village of Elmira" in 1808. Finally, the "Village of Elmira" became the "City of Elmira" in 1864. Therefore, although we are celebrating Elmira's Sesquicentennial, white people have lived here about 231 years.

Settlers began arriving in 1788, a whole year before New York State had legal title from the Iroquois. Surveyors scoured the area and established jurisdictional boundaries. They designated and numbered 205 tracts of land. Each tract was "more than 100 acres" and "less than 1,000 acres." Each acre cost "one shilling and a six-pence." A local militia organized to protect new settlers from each other and possible Indian retaliations.

Colonel John Hendy, born in Wyoming, Pennsylvania in 1757, was one of the first settlers to claim land in Elmira. He fought in the Revolutionary War in the battles of Princeton, Trenton, and others. Hendy canoed up the Chemung River from Athens, Pennsylvania in the spring of 1788 and moved his family here in the fall. Hendy planted corn immediately after his arrival. He built a shanty at "Hendytown," near today's Rorick's Glen Parkway. His family, on their first night in Elmira, complained of howling wolves around the shanty.

John Hendy was a friend to the local Native Americans. They called him "Shi-na-w-ane" meaning "Great Warrior." Hendy was six-foot-seven-inches tall with long, flowing hair. Indians frequently visited the Hendy cabin as overnight guests. Most were friendly, but one attempted to kill him in his sleep. John Hendy fought back and survived the attack.

A terrible famine in August 1790 followed a severe summer frost. The Hendy family's crops froze. They had no money and nothing to eat. They boiled green pumpkins and mashed them with milk. This was not enough to survive. Weeks later a neighbor divided his premature rye crop among the hungry settlers. Mrs. Hendy baked a rye cake and fed it to her nearly starved husband and children. They recovered.

John Hendy dug the first shovelful of dirt for the Chemung Canal in 1830. He died in 1840 and was buried in the "Old Wisner Cemetery"

– the eastern part of today's Wisner Park. When Woodlawn Cemetery opened in 1858, Hendy's body was moved to it. He was the first person buried there. John W. Jones was in charge of Hendy's re-interment. According to a Park Church lecture, Jones once said, "I found [Hendy's] skeleton all complete and the hair was long and beautiful, white, and wavy. I took it up and hung it in my hands like a perfect wig. The men that watched me said it was wonderful." Jones then carefully placed the hair at the head of the skeleton and it was sealed in Hendy's new coffin. A long procession of military, firemen and civic societies accompanied Hendy's body to Woodlawn Cemetery.

And don't worry about Wisner Park today - all 250 human remains were re-interred by John W. Jones to Woodlawn Cemetery in 1877.

The *Telegram* fire of 1913. Photograph courtesy of the Eleanor Barnes Library.

Telegram Fire of 1913

by James Hare

H arry J. Brooks was in Del Monte, California for the winter. He and two partners, Charles Hazzard and James Hill, had founded the *Sunday Telegram*, publishing its first edition on the first Sunday in May of 1879. They had contributed $25 each, and for a total of $75 began one of the first Sunday papers outside of the large cities. Their creation was successful because at that time New York Sunday papers were unable to be delivered early enough to compete. The *Telegram* was the first newspaper in Elmira to be equipped with the mechanical printer which provided its Associated Press dispatches direct from New York to the Elmira offices without a person involved. In 1889, the *Telegram* became the first newspaper in the country to produce two or more colors on a web press that was built for black ink only. Between 1900 and 1910 its circulation averaged 200,000 customers. The paper reflected the "energy and grit" of its owners.

By March of 1913, Brooks was the sole proprietor of the *Sunday Telegram*. His vacation was interrupted by a telegram reporting the events of Thursday, March 13th. "*Telegram* burned, nothing saved. Are we through or shall we continue?" Brooks replied, "Quit? Never! Order new equipment. Will start for home at once."

The fire referred to in the message broke out in the Amusu Theater building on State Street at 6:10PM. Exactly where and how it started would be questioned when it was all over. News reports stated that, "the burned area covers the space bounded by Market Street on the north, State Street on the west, Exchange Place on the east and the rear of the buildings facing on Nicks Street on the south. The buildings burned were the Elmira *Telegram*, the N.J. Thompson dry goods store, the Amusu Theater and the Thomas F. Connelly building...." Estimates of damage ranged from $300,000 to $350,000 (seven to eight million dollars in 2015 dollars).

Apparently the fire began in the rear of the Amusu Theater. It was a one-story wooden structure originally built as a skating rink. At the time of the fire it had been converted into a theater where moving pictures were shown. According to reports, "the theater building was as good as lost" before the firemen reached the fire. So great was the intensity of the flames, the firemen were driven back and their efforts to keep the fire in the theater building failed. The fire spread quickly through to the *Telegram* building and, "in almost an instant the rear end of that building was a mass of flames, which seemed to leap and spread out like the leaves of a flower."

A second alarm was issued within a half hour of the first with every piece of apparatus in the city responding. The departments from Elmira Heights and Horseheads also responded to the call. The American LaFrance Fire Engine Company sent over a motor pumper. "All night they worked valiantly and it is to their credit that they confined the flames in the buildings in which they did," reported the Elmira *Star-Gazette*. The paper noted that, "thousands of people from this city, carloads from Corning, Wellsburg, Horseheads and Elmira Heights viewed the conflagration until a late hour. The streets in the immediate vicinity of the fire were jammed with people and the entire police department was called out to take care of the crowds."

The fire occurred at a most unfortunate time. Half of the fire department was at supper. Only a few men were at the central station while the other four stations were more seriously handicapped by the lack of men. Citizens aided in the work of laying hose.

In the spirit of Harry Brooks, the *Telegram* was issued on Sunday as usual. The *Star-Gazette* offered the use of its plant. Linotype machines of both the *Star-Gazette* and the *Advertiser* were used. Most of the typesetting was done in the *Advertiser* composing room as they worked all day Saturday and thru the night. No bill was presented to the *Telegram* for the use of the equipment. The *Telegram* improvised and "stuck grimly to business as usual." In the Fall of 1913, they moved into a new building at Second and Baldwin Streets.

The *Telegram* fire raised many questions which resulted in an investigation conducted by Mayor Daniel Sheehan and Fire Commissioners Shieve and Wynne. The March 30th *Telegram* headlines read, "Startling Disclosures Made In Regards To Recent Fire Fighting." Testimony and questions were heard from Fire Chief John H. Espey, Harry M. Beardsley, the general manager of the Elmira Water, Light and Railroad Company, Fenton B. Weaver an insurance agent and Thomas F. Connelly, a grocer, as well as others.

Among issues raised was the unsafe condition of the ladder on the "Hayes Truck." Apparently it "was not in such a condition that the chief of the department would order men to mount it... as it swayed and was considered dangerous." Mayor Sheehan noted that it was "general talk of the city that Elmira has good ground firemen and they were not so good when off the ground." Another concern was that it had been "two or three months" since the captains of the different companies had met to discuss fire fighting and fire conditions. Record keeping raised questions when it was shown that the exact time that the firemen leave the headquarters to go to lunch or on errands was not recorded. Lack of judgement on the part of some members or officials of the department was questioned regarding the attachment of the largest and best steamer to a hydrant with a 6-inch water main when 8- and 10-inch mains were accessible.

Chief Espey stated that streams of water "become weak when so many lines of hose are attached." Mr. Beardsley made the case that there was an "ample supply of water." Mayor Sheehan remarked that "up to this time there had been no complaint of the lack of water at the time of the fire." There were questions about the type of hose used and why was water thrown on the burning theater when it was clear the old wood building could not be saved.

The investigation was thorough and one result was the Mayor announced that the city would "probably" purchase a new piece of apparatus along with a new aerial truck.

In 1921, the *Telegram* was sold to Rafael R. Govin of Havana, Cuba. He also purchased the *Advertiser*. The two newspapers were moved into one building.

By 1923, the *Telegram* had lost its unique position in the Sunday field. Both the *Telegram* and the *Advertiser* joined the Gannett organization in 1923.

Kanaweola and Adelaide T. Moe

by Diane Janowski

Historians often go looking for something, and find serendipity on their way. This is a story of one of those journeys.

I started my quest with the name of a gruesome tale - *Kanaweola* meaning "severed head on a pole." Along the way, I discovered a poet and suffragette born and raised Elmira.

According to Seneca legend, Kanaweola was one of seven Native American villages in our county. Red Jacket, the Seneca orator and Chief of the Wolf Clan, sent couriers to the Five Nations of the Iroquois, and in autumn 1730 convened a council at Pine Plains. This was a well-known place of assembly near the confluence of the Chemung River and Newtown Creek (Water Street at Interstate 86 at the eastern boundary of Elmira). At this council, a chief, whose name has not survived history, was convicted for alleged treachery to his tribe and decapitated. His head was placed on a pole as a warning to others. In derision, the place was called Ka-na-we-o-la. Out of superstition, the Native Americans avoided this place.

At one time, the village had twenty well-built houses. The village was destroyed by General John Sullivan's army in 1779. Years later when white settlers came this locality was called She-ne-do-wa meaning "at the great plains." The first name given to the settlement by the whites was Newtown or Newtown Point. "Pine Plains" encompassed the area of today's Elmira, Big Flats, and Horseheads.

While researching Kanaweola, I discovered a small book of verse, Owenah: A Legend of Kanaweola written in 1875 in Elmira by Adelaide T. Moe. I wanted to know, who was Adelaide and what was her connection to Kanaweola?

As it turns out, Adelaide T. (Reynolds) Moe was born in 1830 in Elmira to Isaac and Jane Reynolds. Isaac brought his family to Southport from Westchester County in 1825. He was a boat builder, and later

OWENAH:

A LEGEND OF KANAWEOLA.

(THE INDIAN NAME OF ELMIRA.)

ELMIRA, N. Y.
ADVERTISER ASSOCIATION, PRINTERS.
1875.

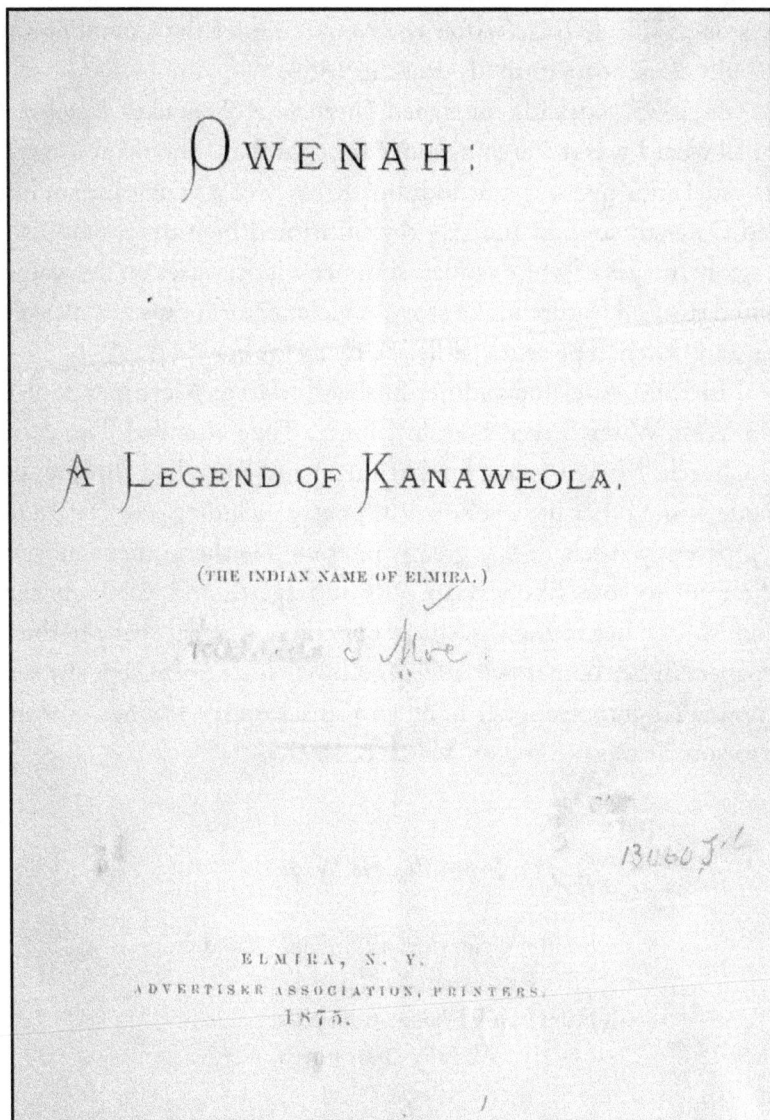

Title page of Adelaide's book, *Owenah: A Legend of Kanaweola*.

a lumberman. He frequently shipped lumber, salt, plaster, and grain down the Chemung and Susquehanna rivers to points south, and was known at every stop as "Uncle Isaac." After the completion of the Chemung Canal, Isaac built canal boats until his death in 1865.

In 1875, Adelaide published *Owenah: A Legend of Kanaweola* – not at all what I was researching, but I thought that I should at least check it out. Adelaide's poem is a melodramatic story of a young Indian hunter named Owenah, and an Indian princess named Newamee, who lived in our region. Images of white canoes, summer winds, waves on the water, the "haunted tree," all feature in the story. A violent storm capsizes Newamee's canoe, and Owenah perishes while searching for her.

In 1880, Adelaide and her husband Marcus Mortimer Moe lived at 143 West Water Street, here in Elmira. They attended Trinity Episcopal Church. Marcus was a lumber merchant. They had three children. Adelaide wrote other little volumes of poetry including *The Old Fountain Inn*. Apparently, Adelaide was greatly interested in the women's movement for the right to vote. She was an early suffragette, and although her life and family took her to Kansas, she frequently sent poems back to the local newspapers in her hometown. Here is a lovely little poem that she sent to the Elmira *Telegram* from her home in Kansas on her feelings of women's right to vote. It was printed on March 8, 1891.

From Prairie Wide

From prairie wide, from mountainside;
From forest, field and glade,
From humble home, from palace dome,
"We rally undismayed.

Yes, we're coming, brother, coming.
Full a hundred thousand strong;
We're coming to sit down and talk.
And tarry with you long.

"We're women, only women,
But our cares we'll leave at home,
And look the very best we can,
So you'll be glad we've come.

And so we'll just politely ask
The ballot at your hand,
By right 'tis ours; you'll not deny
Or slight our pleading band.

Just set the suffrage question right.
And keep it there apace.
And we shall vote right heartily,
Nor mind a fool's grimace.

Suppose 'twere not exactly right,
(Though right it was we trow)
But give it pray, we ask so sweet
And womanly you know.

We'll put our prettiest foot before
For so men like us better,
Adverse they may construe the law,
By vote we'll "point the letter."

Sources:

Elmira *Telegram*, March 8, 1891

History of Tioga, Chemung, Tompkins and Schuyler counties, New York: with illustrations and biographical sketches of some of its prominent men and pioneers. Philadelphia: Everts & Ensign/J. B. Lippincott, 1879.

The Children's Reconstruction Home

by James Hare

Officials of the Home were presented to the Governor while the inmates cheered the State's chief executive. Then the official car was backed into the driveway of the Home and several of the crippled children were greeted personally by Governor Roosevelt. He had a pleasant greeting for every child presented. To one he said, "How's the arm?" to another, "How is the leg coming along?" Only one brace now, I see. He compared his own illness to one patient he met." (Elmira *Advertiser* August 14, 1929) The Elmira *Star-Gazette* noted that "at first the youngsters who could walk with crutches were reticent about getting up to speak to the Governor of New York State. But, when Roosevelt smiled, they all hobbled up to meet him... even the youngsters who were helpless in their cots asked to meet him...."

The Children's Reconstruction Home was located at 563 Maple Avenue. Governor Roosevelt responded to an invitation while in Elmira to inspect the "Reformatory." "I have always wanted to see the Elmira home. It is similar to the one I am now operating in Warm Springs, Georgia, he said." (*Star-Gazette* August 14, 1929). Five years before, Roosevelt was stricken with polio, in 1921. The paralyzing disease struck thousands in the United States, killing 6,000. During the 1916 epidemic 9,000 cases were reported in New York City. Mark Sauer, a polio survivor noted in *A Paralyzing Fear* that, "there were many other diseases that were bad for America, but polio broke its heart." The Children's Reconstruction Home was a project of the Elmira Rotary Club. The doors opened July 22, 1923. By the end of the year twenty one children had been admitted to the Home.

The plight of "crippled" children had been of interest to several Rotary members prior to December 1921 when Edgar F. Allen, President of the National Society of Crippled Children, came to Elmira to address the Elmira Club on the work for crippled children. At that time there was no public agency in the state to look after the welfare of children who were

THE TELEGRAM, DECEMBER 28, 192⅘.

Christmas Tree For Crippled Children

Youngsters at Reconstruction Home on Maple avenue forget their pain and worries in the excitement and enjoyment provided
y Christmas festivities arranged by the members of the Rotary Club. There were nice presents for all and these were distributed
y Santa Claus (himself). The grown-up were provided as much joy as the youngsters in the gift of glad and happy smiles be-
owed upon them by the little children in the Home.

Photo from the Elmira *Advertiser*, December 28, 1928

tormented with some physical defect. "In many cases they were neglected and were going without the advantage of medical care, an education or encouragement."

According to a local Rotary history, in August of 1922, President "Tom" Bolger appointed a committee to look into the advisability of the Club taking up the work. The committee decided to evaluate the need in the county. A canvass of the county was made, resulting in eighty-two children brought in to a two day clinic. Information learned from the clinic provided "proof" of the need for work on behalf of crippled children on a large scale in the vicinity of Elmira.

At a meeting on January 19, 1923, the Club unanimously accepted the responsibility and before the meeting adjourned about $15,200 was subscribed by the members for the work. The Rotary Anns (the wives of Rotary members) organized on January 10, 1923, contributed to the supervision and furnishing of the Home. The Club purchased the former home of Governor Lucius Robinson on Maple Avenue. The *Sunday Telegram* reported January 26, 1924 that, "the home of the governor and his lady has undergone many changes... the laughter of children is still present, but the dancing feet are missing. Instead is heard the thump, thump, thump of a crutch, roll of a wheel chair, the faltering limp of a lame child."

George Personius, a leading proponent of the Home and a member of the Finance Committee presented the first report on the Home's activities. He noted that, "inside are three large wards, two exercise rooms, a fine school room, six rooms for the superintendent and assistants, ten fire places, four bath rooms, dining room, kitchen and laundry...." The Board of Education completely furnished the school room and also supplied the grade and high school teacher.

The Rotary Anns placed the first child in the Home at a cost of $450. Albert Roy gave the Home a pedigreed calf which sold for $300 at the Rotary auction. Personius noted that the public was supporting the Home, "during the last six months 170 persons have donated a large quantity of miscellaneous supplies and the same number have signed the visitor register."

Miss Nelda King was the first superintendent, with seventeen children ranging from four to seventeen years of age under her care. Burton

C. Meeker, president of the Meeker Business Institute and president of the Home, wanted Elmirans to "get the habit" of visiting, according to the *Telegram*. If the visitors stay a few moments, Harry Hutchinson, "the 250-pound superintendent of schools will walk in on a tour of inspection. The tour is just an excuse of Harry's to say Hello to the kids and to pass out the sunny smile that would almost bring to life a 3,000 year old mummy."

The Children's Reconstruction Home officially closed its doors on January 19, 1937. State agencies were becoming more involved providing education and medical care. In the years between 1923-1937 approximately 350 children were treated and cared for at the Home. In January of 1985, the Home, which had become a multifamily apartment house, was severely damaged by fire and demolished in August of that year.

Frostilla
FRAGRANT LOTION

It Is So Delightful To Use

Many women and men prefer Frostilla Fragrant Lotion, because it is so easy and pleasant to use. It refreshes the skin immediately and leaves no stickiness. All that remains is a delicate fragrance which is the blend of many lovely flowers.

Frostilla Fragrant Lotion is wonderful for Sunburn and Windburn. It quickly soothes away all pain and leaves a cooling feeling of comfort. It cleanses the pores of dust; it prevents the skin from cracking or growing dry. In fact, you will find Frostilla Fragrant Lotion almost indispensable all through the year for skin attractiveness.

Before powdering use Frostilla Fragrant Lotion as a foundation. Then notice how smoothly the powder goes on and how long it clings. After the use of a depilatory a little Frostilla Fragrant Lotion will prevent the slightest irritation.

There are many other uses such as: to refresh tired feet, to stop chafing and to soften the cuticle in manicuring. You will be constantly finding new needs for it after you have once tried it.

In Shaving: After shaving Frostilla Fragrant Lotion takes away all sting and soreness. A little dropped on the wet, soapy brush will not only foam up the lather, but help to soften the beard.

For sale everywhere—regular price 35 cents. The Frostilla Company. Elmira, N. Y.

Frostilla advertisement in the Los Angeles *Times* (Los Angeles, California) July 2, 1922 page 133.

Made in Elmira and Chemung County

by Diane Janowski

Over the years many fine products have been made locally. If you grew up here you learned about our fire hydrants, coaster brakes, fire engines, friction clutches, glass bottles, machine tools, TV tubes, greeting cards, typewriters, cut flowers, boxes and packaging materials. But, you may not know that there were many other products, now obsolete, that were made right here.

If you were a sick child with chest congestion and a cough back in 1909, your mother might have "greased" you with "Brown's Eucalyptus Ointment." It smelled strong but the manufacturer, William S. Gerity of Gerity's Drug Store on Lake Street, claimed it worked.

Another concoction made here was internationally-known fragrant pink lotion called "Frostilla." The Frostilla company was founded on Lake Street in 1884 by Clay Holmes. After a terrible fire he moved his production to 410 West Gray Street – the Madame Halina dance studio building. The business continued under Holmes' son-in-law, Floyd Shoemaker after Holmes death. The business was sold in 1949 to the Wildroot Company of Buffalo.

Peter Biggs' father, Michael, came from Ireland to Elmira in the early 1830s to help dig the Chemung Canal. Peter soon followed and saw the opportunity to help keep Elmirans clean. Peter Biggs opened the Elmira Steam Soap Works making good old-fashioned soap. The soap was boiled by steam for four days, drawn and run into frames, then cut into bars in the required size. Because his business was at an important location near Elmira's Junction Canal, he was able to easily load his products onto canal boat and ship them to all points from Seneca Lake, and Pennsylvania. His factory was on the southeast corner of Madison Avenue and East Fifth Street. It was razed after being severely damaged by the July 2012 tornado.

In 1837, John M. Robinson owned the Robinson Chair Company. He made cottage chairs, Boston rocking chairs, and Windsor chairs. His city directory advertisement said that his business was located, "A few doors below the bridge, opposite the Chemung Canal Bank."

Elmira even had several mattress manufacturers in the late 1800s. The biggest local company was the Queen City Mattress Company at 620 State Street. Their mattresses were made with "Hair, Cotton, Wool, Fibre, Husk, or Grass Excelsior." Another company F. M. Blystone made "Downyrest" mattresses at 744 Baldwin Street in 1894.

The Elmira Knitting Mill in Elmira Heights produced knitwear including sweaters, socks, hats, and scarves from 1893 to 1963. During World War II they produced clothing for the military. Another mill was the Campbell Knitting Mill at 821 East Avenue in the heart of Frog Hollow neighborhood. In 1904 the company employed 225 workers. Wool underwear was their chief product.

L. Freudenheim's factory at 111 Railroad Avenue made women's skirts. In 1905, the company produced around 55,000 skirts a year. It closed in the 1920s. Also on Railroad Avenue from 1880-1908 was the J. Richardson & Company shoe factory that produced 1,600 pairs a week. Mr. Richardson provided homes for his employees and executives in the row houses and apartment buildings on West Water Street at the foot of Davis Street.

In the early 20th century, Elmira was home to several musical instrument factories making pianos and organs. Robert Hope-Jones invented the "modern theater organ" and produced them on Madison Avenue and East Fifth Street. He sold his patents to the Wurlitzer company. Jacob Greener manufactured pianos between 1864 and 1916. William King opened an organ factory on College Avenue from 1865 to 1887. The quaint building still exists just north of Goodyear Tires.

M. Doyle Marks came to Elmira in 1898 and opened a franchised piano store. In 1904, he bought out his obligations to the franchise and renamed the store after himself. Marks designed an upright piano – the "Doylemarx" that sounded good and was affordable to the public. His store closed in the 1930s.

Brothers Daniel and Floyd Hungerford were, among other things, "airplane and airship builders" at 823 West Second Street. In 1909, they

Shirley Lois Moon Girl, research vehicle in 1929, built by brothers Daniel and Floyd Hungerford on Chevrolet chassis mod. 1921 and equipped with auxiliary propulsion rocket. Photo by April Younglove, 2009. This "automobile" is on display at the New York State Museum in Albany.

built their first airplane and flew it at their private airstrip in Southport. Neighbors along Second Street considered the brothers either geniuses or just crazy. In 1929, they built their most famous project the "Rocket Car" around a 1921 Chevrolet auto body. The first test run was on November 2, 1929, when it roared down West Second Street with a twenty-foot flame shooting out behind. Neighbors snickered when they saw it, but it held acclaim in scientific circles. The Rocket Car now resides on display at the New York State Museum in Albany.

Elmira and Chemung County have also produced many good food products. From about 1900 to 1920 Charles Hancock had a bread making plant at 409 Madison Avenue. He made "Hancock's Buster Brown Bread." B.F. McCain's bakery on East Washington Avenue made big pretzels. C.

W. Smith on Baldwin Street provided Elmirans with freshly made crackers in 1886. Every year, father and son Sylvester and Fred Rogers made gallons of maple syrup at their facility at Pigeon Point. Elmira even had two horseradish producers in 1912 – the Taylor brothers, W.H. and H. on Judson Street, and Nickolas Viele on Harper Street provided the piquant sauce for Elmira's roast beef.

Cigar manufacturers were dotted all over town. T.O Shannon made fine cigars at 514 North Main Street in 1894. Some of his brands were "Reliana" and "City Club." Competitor William Hart of 603 Lake Street made "Country Club" and "Two Harts." At 376 South Main Street, John C. Conlon made "Feast of the Flowers."

Reliance Motorcycle Works in Elmira Heights produced motorcycle engines in 1900. One of the company's mechanics was Glenn Curtiss of Hammondsport who helped make the best machines possible.

For medicinal purposes there was "Old Lowman Whiskey." The distillery in Lowman closed around 1918 with the advent of prohibition. If that was too strong, Calvin Johnson produced "Standard Malted Milk" in his Grove Street home from 1933-1936.

Other liquid product manufactures include the Eagle Bottling Works at 420 Carroll Street, who in 1901 were famous for their apple cider, birch beer, cream soda, chocolate soda, and lemon sour soda.

So remember – Elmira and Chemung County have been the home of many products thanks to the ingenuity of our local citizens. In 2015, fire hydrants, friction clutches, boxes and packaging materials are still being made locally.

The Elmira College Observatory

by James Hare

Observatory. [Elmira Female College] Photographer C. Tomlinson, circa 1868. Courtesy of The Miriam and Ira D. Wallach Division of Art, Prints and Photographs: Photography Collection.

"On November 14, 1868 our class in astronomy took our positions about the dome of the Observatory. We divided the heavens into ten sections, with the stipulation that each girl should count only the meteors which seemed to originate in her section, in order to avoid duplication. About 11 P.M. a perfect *Kappa Sigma* appeared in the northwest, quite a proper thing to do as we were all members of the

Kappa Sigma sorority. From that time the meteors came thick and fast and we counted over five thousand till the rising sun obscured their view. Dr. Ford, of blessed memory, furnished us with 'eats' and blankets, for it certainly was frosty that November night." (the reminiscence of a meteor shower seen by Elmira College girls in 1868 by Mary C. Davis, Class of 1869).

The seniors sat up all night at the Observatory. The freshmen were to be awakened by a bell when the shower began. They were advised to wear "heavy gowns" and to go wherever they liked to see the show. "Of course no one slept much, and when the bell rang we were out in a jiffy, slipped into our clothes, grabbed a comfortable blanket and away we went... Such a sight! I have never seen anything like it since... it was a joyous astronomy class who strolled home about 4 A.M. and had the right to sleep all that day." So wrote Mrs. Nora Stanford Wills, Class of 1873. She went on to record, "When '73's turn came, all the usual preparations were made, but there wasn't a star to be seen, and after vainly trying all the instruments, we ate our spread and trooped back and were in bed by eleven o'clock."

The Elmira College Observatory was located at Sixth Street and Park Place, where the Elmira College book store is currently located. Ground was broken on August 8, 1859 and the building went into service April 1, 1860. According to *Elmira College The First 100 Years*, the Observatory was built because Professor Charles S. Farrar was "both astronomer and a go-getter."

The Observatory had its beginning in 1858, when Farrar borrowed a 4-inch refractor from S.C. Camp of Owego. Students were so interested, that an attempt was made to buy it for $275, but failed. Apparently, Professor Farrar did not let the idea drop and in February, 1859, the purchase of a 6-inch telescope was completed. Then when an 8-inch telescope became available for $1,600, Farrar bought it with an "$800 chattel mortgage" as part of the deal. With the acquisition of the telescope, Farrar began a campaign to raise $3,000 to build the Observatory. The college trustees, "didn't welcome to the campus any addition that was darkened by an eclipse of debt," so an on campus location was not available. However, E. P. Brooks offered to donate the triangle of land at Park Place and Sixth Street which Farrar accepted. The funds for the project were raised by private subscription. The Academy of Science was founded in 1861, with the Reverend Thomas K. Beecher as its first president. The Academy operated the Observatory for nearly two decades before turning it over to the college.

Alisha Kingsbury drew the plans for what the *Callisophia* (a bimonthly published by the Elmira Female College) September-October 1860 described as "26-foot cube with symmetrical wings for Transit Room and Library, and mounted with an octagonal observing room and revolving dome." Attached to the Observatory was a two story structure with a "spacious auditorium capable of seating 150 persons." The Academy of Science would meet in the auditorium. On the second floor was a museum used for geological exhibits.

The opening of the Observatory caused a "scramble on the part of Elmirans to have a peek... these were permitted to buy 'gazing stock,' which entitled them to a glimpse now and then at the stars, charged against their donations... others paid a fee of 25 cents for the privilege... the rush began!..." (Elmira *Star-Gazette*, June 29, 1939).

After 1928-29, the Elmira College catalogue no longer contained descriptions of the Observatory. It had fallen into disuse and ill repair. The decision was made to demolish the building in 1939. According to *Elmira College the First 100 Years*, "It passed on before the nation's juke boxes issued strident warnings against letting the stars get in your eyes."

The *Elmira History and Directory, 1868*, noted that the longitude of the Observatory was 76 degrees 48' 28" West of Greenwich and its latitude was 42 degrees 6' 25" North... It was about exactly on the meridian of the National Observatory of Washington.

The Name Game

By Diane Janowski

Chemung County's communities and neighborhoods have had their share of offbeat names over the last 250 years.

Chemung, NY was first called "Buckville" after Elijah Buck. Chemung Center was first called "Beantown" after its postmaster Daniel Bean.

Horseheads was "Horseheads" in 1779, then "Fairport" in 1837, then "Horseheads" again in 1845, then "North Elmira" in 1886, in 1887 the citizens voted on a final name by a margin of 208 to 199 for it to be "Horseheads."

In 1822, two pieces of Elmira were taken off to form the towns of Big Flats and Southport. Early, Big Flats was called "Great Plains," and sometimes "Little Egypt." "Southport" was designated for the port of rafts and boats on the south side of the Chemung River.

Lowman was first called "West Chemung" and "Stumptown." Later it was renamed for Jacob Lowman. Millport was "Millvale" in 1828. Pine City was "Pine Woods" in 1830. Wellsburg had an "h" at the end of its name until 1872. Until 1822, Erin was "Erin-Go-Bragh" for its Irish inhabitants.

Neighborhoods in Elmira had their own names, too. "Pigeon Point" at Lake and Oak Streets was known as a home for thousands of pigeons. "Frog Hollow," east of Madison and north of Church and south of Harper was known for its swampy land. "Pickaway" on the Southside, was named for its stony soil and settled by many Irish families. Now, it is the site of Saints Peter & Paul cemetery.

"The Buttonwoods" was the area east of Brand Park named for the "buttonball" or sycamore trees that grow there. Its inhabitants were German and Irish. "The Irish Patch" was near the Rolling Mill on East Washington Avenue and first inhabited by the English, Irish, and the Welsh.

"The Italian Patch" neighborhood included Railroad Avenue, Magee, and North Main Streets, and part of Washington Avenue. The Southside had a "Patch," too. Irish immigrants lived in the area of today's Tops Market.

Advertisement for the Pigeon Point Launder Service. Elmira *Advertiser* (Elmira, New York) January 8, 1959 page 12.

"Slabtown" was an Eastside neighborhood near today's Jones Court. It took its name from the housing construction that used wooden planks one foot wide. Former slaves who came north seeking a better life originally settled there and built many homes and four churches.

The Bragg Towers area was commonly known by the derogatory name "Jewtown." It had many fine homes and several temples. "German-town" existed around Madison Avenue and East Church Streets. "Polander-town" extended from College Avenue to the Arnot Ogden Medical Center and from Washington Avenue to the Elmira Correctional Facility.

Elmira Heights' first name was the "Industrial Association Grounds" before 1896. Residents voted for a better name and from 93 votes – 56 were for "Elmira Heights," 32 were for "New Elmira," and 3 for "Elmira High-lands."

The "Carr's Corners" area was once quite lively. Today, the area is the five-corner stop at West Hill Road, Hoffman Street, Bancroft Road, and Hillcrest Road.

The "Brookside Gardens" neighborhood opened in 1917. It included Sherman, Plymouth, and Woodbine Avenues.

"Universal Village" on Robert and Allen Streets provided homes for the Remington-Rand employees.

Elmira College sits at the top of the former Prospect Hill. The area was a large prospective development along College Avenue all the way to Mary Street, and east to the railroad tracks and west to Davis Street.

Back in the old days, an unwritten law kept groups in their own neighborhoods in the early days of immigration. Today, the former immigrant groups are interspersed in all levels of society. I found a few neighborhood names today – "Five Corners" is the area formerly known as Carr's Corners, the "Point" is in West Elmira at Church and Water, and "WOHO" is the shopping/eating area on the west side of Hoffman Street. Families of inmates at the correctional facilities commonly refer to Elmira as "E-Block" or "E-town."

**BEN HUR
IS HERE**

———

Religio-Dramatic Spec-
tacle at the Lyceum
Theater.

———

SPLENDID
      PERFORMANCE

Elmira *Gazette and Free Press*, March 30, 1906 page 8.

The Lyceum

by James Hare

T he *Evening Star* headline for Friday, March 30, 1906 read, *"Ben Hur Beyond All Anticipation, Magnificent Production of Massive, Impressive and Thrilling Play at the Lyceum Last Night—Triumph."*

When first announced, there were "predictions" of empty houses for the production. But those predictions were proved wrong. Ben-Hur became the "talk of the city." It was reported that folks regretted not getting tickets for a second show because it was "so comprehensive, absorbingly interesting and positively thrilling."

The chariot race between Massala and Ben-Hur was described as a distinct "triumph of stage realism." Two Roman chariots drawn by "eight blooded steeds" dashed headlong across the stage. "It was no timed, tame, stupid stage race, but a dashing, daring, startling contest which brought many of the audience to their feet," the newspaper reported. Chemung County Historian Tom Byrne noted that it was all made possible by a "noisy treadmill."

The Lyceum, which began as the Opera House has been called "Elmira's greatest theater" according to W. Charles Barber in a 1952 *Star-Gazette* article about Elmira's "famous theaters of yesteryear."

In the mid 1860's Elmira was a thriving village with a growing reputation and would become a city in 1864. Reportedly, there were "an unusually large number of men above the average intelligence," who conceived the development of an entire block.

Silas Haight and his son in law Dr. Henry H. Purdy secured three parcels of land on Lake, Market and Carroll Streets on November 30, 1864 for "purposes of speculation." A variety of investors bought and sold parcels until Henry S. Gilbert and Daniel R. Platt formed the Lake Street Building Association in 1866. Their purpose was to erect "a public hall of suit-

LYCEUM THEATER Monday, October 8th

M. REIS, Manager,

Direct from its phenomenal run of seven months in New York.

ALFRED E. AARONS'

MERRY MUSICAL SUCCESS

"HIS HONOR THE MAYOR"

With Harry Kelly as Deacon Flood, the Original English Ponies, and the entire New York cast of 100 persons—mostly charming girls.

PRICES—$1.50, $1.00, 75c, 50c and 25c. 600 seats at 25c for the biggest and best show Elmira has known in years.

Elmira Gazette & Free Press October 8, 1906 page 6.

able style and capacity commensurate with the growth and prosperity of the city... at some central and convenient place in such city...."

The Opera House block, at Lake and Carroll Streets (where the Five Star Bank is currently located) would be one of the most "imposing business blocks in Elmira," following the Civil War. There would be two buildings in the development. The Opera House would occupy the upper floors of one building with seven stores underneath. It would cost $89,000 when ready for occupancy. Its main entrance was from Lake Street with a side entrance off of Carroll Street. Capacity, when full, was 2,000. It opened on December 17, 1867 with a lecture by John B. Gough on temperance with over 1,000 people attending. According to the newspaper, audience comments ranged from "Isn't it splendid, beautiful and the whole vocabulary of adjectives was exhausted, upon many graceful as well as manly lips."

The Opera House brought "topflight" productions to Elmira.

Two years after performing for President Lincoln at Ford's Theater, Laura Keene appeared in "Our American Cousin." Edwin Booth, the brother of Lincoln's assassin was on stage in "Julius Caesar." Samuel L. Clemens (Mark Twain) "spoke from the stage... in 1868 while courting Olivia Langdon. His topic, according to Tom Byrne was, "The American Vandal Abroad."

Extending down Lake Street toward Water Street, separated by a twelve-foot alley, would be five "magnificent" stores on the first floor and "splendid" apartments above. It would cost $95,000 to construct this second building in the new development.

In 1894, Colonel David C. Robinson, the son of former governor Lucius Robinson, and a former mayor of Elmira, acquired the Opera House. He remodeled the building and it was renamed the Lyceum in 1898. In the old house there were no boxes, but a gallery encircled two-thirds of the auditorium. The remodeling placed two boxes in tiers on each side and shortened the gallery.

On Sunday, March 6, 1904 the theater was entirely destroyed by fire caused by an explosion in one of the stores underneath as the "playhouse was on the second floor back." It was a huge fire with the business section of Elmira, at that time, "threatened with destruction" according to Insurance Engineering. Two theaters and six stores were burned with property damage estimated at $175,000.

On October 19, 1905, the New Lyceum, as it was called, re-opened.

The Elmira *Gazette* reported that, "it is doubtful if there is a finer theater outside of New York or Chicago and the stage is one of the largest ever built." The opening production was a comic opera called the "Isle of Spice" and restored "winter theater" to Elmira for the first time since the fire.

Charles Barber observed that "some of the theater's greatest days were seen near the end of its career." Those were the days when John Golden built his shows in Elmira before taking them to Broadway. Nearly a dozen shows, i.e. "Seventh Heaven," "Three Wise Fools," and "Turn to the Right," were born on the Lyceum stage. The curtain, for the Lyceum, came down for the final time in 1926. Barber wrote in the November 27, 1949 *Telegram*, "With the tackle the workmen attached, the arch was pulled down and a column of historic dust rose high in the air. It was the dust of plaster, bricks and mortar which had echoed to the greatest voices and the finest music the stage had to offer and the applause of Elmirans lucky enough to have lived when the Lyceum was in its heyday."

"TEDDY" VISITS THE QUEEN CITY

Made Addresses at the Lyceum and Globe.

AS DID OTHER SPEAKERS.

Colonel Roosevelt Is Not a Pleasing Speaker but Many Gathered to Hear Him—Ex-Senator Fassett Made Happy by Being Made Chairman of the Gathering.

Elmira *Daily Gazette & Free Press* October 25, 1898 page 5.

The Republicans had an inning last night. Theodore Roosevelt and his band of rough riders were in Elmira. There were meetings in the Lyceum and Globe theaters and in the streets, and there were hundreds of people out to see the Republican candidate for governor. "Teddy" was on hand with a train of oratorical followers, and the way the oratory was showered upon unprotected Elmirans was a caution.

It was exactly 8:31 o'clock last evening when "Teddy's" special over the Erie rolled into the depot. Between seventy-five and 100 morbidly curious people, anxious to see what kind of a man "Teddy" was, had assembled on the platform.

There was no band, no escort, and but one lone stick of red fire sent to the depot by the Republican county committee and the small boy in charge had ignited said stick when the train first came into view with the result that "Teddy" and his half dozen "Tough Riders" arrived in darkness, the "pyrotechnic display" having burned itself out.

The One Hundred Block of North Main Street in the 1920's

by James Hare

The obituary read,

"For 48 long and serviceable years the old iron structure has furnished the way for pedestrians and vehicles to cross and re-cross the Chemung in ceaseless numbers. But alas, the vigorous march of progress has shoved aside the faithful servant, the back of which has borne the weight of ten million people since its' construction during the reconstruction period following the Civil War. Through the steady march of feet, hoofs, wheels and the consuming decay of time, the ancient bridge was condemned three years ago as unsafe for heavy "traffic."

Five days after this article appeared in the Elmira *Star-Gazette*, on the morning of September 26, 1921 the old steel Main Street bridge, built in 1873, was demolished. It was replaced by a new concrete bridge which many felt was "the greatest improvement Elmira ever enjoyed in a long period."

The new bridge was officially opened on December 26, 1921 with Hager's Band giving an hour long concert beginning at 3PM which was followed by a parade. A platoon of police, Mayor George W. Peck and members of the Common Council led the parade marching across a "prettily decorated structure" from north to the south side. Miss Murial Iszard led the crowd in singing Christmas carols. Jervis Langdon and Mayor Peck were the featured speakers. According to Langdon, "this beautiful bridge which could lift its head (or should I say span) had it been built anywhere among the renown bridges of the world—across the Potomac... the Thames... the Seine... or the Arno at old Florence" capped numbers of handsome structures in Elmira. Mayor Peck noted that, "our bridges unite and make us one community, therefore if we are to prosper, we must have good bridges."

The bridge cost $366,834.95 and had the support of the taxpayers and the business community. It was the third "Main Street bridge and would last until the Flood of 1972. Perhaps more significantly it opened a decade of growth and development for North Main Street.

During the 1920's, Elmira's center of gravity moved west. During and after the Civil War Elmira boomed. Water Street was the "first shopping center" with much of the activity east of Baldwin Street. By the mid 1920's there was so much growth taking place west of Baldwin Street that the city undertook a second major improvement in transportation with proposals to elevate the railroad tracks. Beginning in 1925, at a mass meeting held in the Federation Building, John J. Mitchell, Vice President of the Erie Railroad and Frank Tripp, general manager of the Gannett Newspaper Company raised the issue of elevating the tracks running through the city (when the railroad arrived in 1849 it was west of the city center—in the 1920's that was likened to having the railroad run along Hoffman Street.) The following year on Saturday, April 27, 1926 a seven-hour traffic survey was conducted on Water Street at the Erie crossing. With a "regular checking machine" pedestrians who crossed the tracks between 11:30AM and 6:30 PM were counted and the amount of time they were delayed by train traffic was tabulated. During that period 18,776 people crossed the Erie track with Elmirans losing thirteen days of aggregate time waiting for trains to pass.

It would be eight more years (1934) before "United Elmira Day" celebrated the elevation of the crossings but the forces of progress noted at the opening of the Main Street bridge were at work.

Certainly, one of the key developments for North Main Street during the 1920s was the bold move by the S. F. Iszard Company to purchase property at 150 North Main Street in 1922. The newspaper described it as "one of the most desirable" properties. It went on to say that "the new Main Street took a big step forward in its efforts for commercial supremacy" when the Iszard Company purchased the Fitzgerald property for $75,000. S. F. Iszard had purchased his original store in 1904 at the corner of East Water and Baldwin Streets. With business growing there was a need for more space. News accounts reported that he had plans to "erect a new building which would be one of the most modern department stores in this section of the country."

The one hundred block of North Main Street, just north of the bridge, was not without business activity when Iszards made their move. On

September 1, 1901 two traveling salesmen for sporting goods houses, Wesley O. Crew and John N. Willys incorporated the Elmira Arms Company and moved it to 117 North Main Street. They became the first automobile dealers in Elmira when they obtained the agency for the Pierce Motorette. They later added the Rambler, Ford, Winton and White Steamer to their stock, which of course also included a complete line of bicycles, guns, fishing tackle and other sporting goods.

The Schweppes, who owned 121-125 North Main Street ran a wallpaper business. In 1911, they had built the Colonial Theater at 123 North Main Street. It was one of the larger houses and seated 1,200 people. Political rallies, legitimate attractions and vaudeville all took the stage at the Colonial. In 1929, it showed *Wings*, the first Academy award winning

Charles Rogers and Clara Bow in "Wings" at Colonial Theater Beginning Sunday, Aug. 26, at 8:30.

Advertisement for the film *Wings* at the Colonial Theater in the Elmira *Star-Gazette* August 20, 1928 page 11.

film. The movie was accompanied by an orchestra and sound effects as well as "the magna screen, a device which allowed the screen to enlarge in all directions when the aerial dogfights were shown."

On December 6, 1926, two years after Iszards had opened their new store the headline of the *Star-Gazette* proclaimed "Elaborate Business Block To Be Erected At Location Leased By Clothing Company" announcing the decision of the owners of the Gorton Company (one of Elmira's leading women's and children's wearing apparel concerns) to acquire the corner of North Main and Water Streets with plans to build a new four- story building. News reports said the unpublished price involved in the 51-year lease was the "greatest in money value, of any lease ever written in the city." George H. Danzig, president of the Blackmore-Danzig Company announced plans to move the Gorton Company from 107 East Water Street to the new location. The distinctive name Gorton Coy would result from a sign painter's mistake. Instead of abbreviating the word "company" in the English fashion with a capital "C" and an underlined lower case "o" and "y" the painter made C-O-Y one word with equal sized letters. The Gorton "COY" would open in 1931.

Within three years of the Gorton lease the new one million dollar, eight story, Mark Twain Hotel opened on the north side of Iszards in 1929. This was an achievement which required Elmirans to have faith in the future of the city, but it faced controversy in the process. Initially there were questions as to why the corner of North Main and Gray Streets had been selected. J. John Hassett, one of the three lead backers of the project, stated that, "the location was the choice of the most prominent hotel men who had considered the matter of a hotel here, among them John S. Hershey, Captain Bo Bo of the American Hotels, representatives of the Associated Hotels and others." The second concern was whether or not the city should spend $100,000 to widen Gray Street on the Wisner Park side to facilitate traffic. A public referendum was held in which a majority of taxpayers voted no. There was also a public hearing where business men, members of the First Baptist Church and interested citizens spoke for and against the project, many objecting to interfering with the layout of Wisner Park.

Despite the opposition, the Elmira Common Council authorized the expenditure of $75,000 for street widening. The action came about after Mr. and Mrs. J. John Hassett placed in escrow the deed for a strip of land 169-feet long and 17-feet wide from the proposed hotel property valued at $27,000 at no cost to the city. Once this hurdle was overcome the challenge of raising the one million dollars for construction was undertaken. The Association of Commerce, led by Frederic H. Hill undertook a public hotel bond campaign. The plan had been in the works for a while and raised $303,800 from 450 subscribers, critics as well as supporters. Metropolitan Life Insurance took $400,000 worth and Hassett put up the property valued at $150,000 and paid $150,000 in cash.

The Mark Twain Hotel opened in 1929. It became the "Queen of the Queen City". The newspaper noted that "in addition to being a decided asset to Elmira, the Mark Twain will awaken the people to a realization of the possibilities of faith in public achievements. It is a real step forward in the city's progress". At the opening banquet, comments proved that the outside of the hotel made an impression all its own.

Lighted from top to bottom with strains of the orchestra floating faintly from the lobby out over Wisner Park, it made people say, "Gee, Elmira is a great town after all."

Construction of the Mark Twain Hotel in 1928/1929. Photograph courtesy of the Eleanor Barnes Library.

Elmira's Silk Mill

By Diane Janowski

Silk became an important industry in Elmira at the turn of the 20th century. In 1880 the heart of the silk industry was Paterson, New Jersey. When labor relations fell apart, mill owners began looking for other locations that had a large supply of low-cost labor to tend the new machines that were changing the way in silk was spun, knitted, and woven. That location was the Lehigh Valley in Pennsylvania. The coalmines and heavy industries of eastern Pennsylvania were providing work for immigrant men, whose wives and children were available to work in silk mills.

The first mill in Allentown was a success, and soon communities all over the Valley were hoping to lure or create a silk mill. By 1914, the Lehigh Valley was the silk manufacturing center of the world. One of the mills that left Paterson in the 1887 was Read and Lovatt who opened a factory in Weatherly, PA, outside of Hazleton. They opened a second factory in Elmira and a third in Palmerton, PA. The Weatherly operation was the largest spinning mill in the US at the time.

Jerome C. Read was president of Read & Lovatt, and was the president of the Silk Association of America from 1910-1913. He started the business in Elmira in 1887 in the abandoned Barnett Mill at Madison and Fifth Streets. Read & Lovatt began operations with 40 employees. Any boy or girl, 13 years of age or older, could apply for a job at the mill. The owners spent $60,000 for a new building designed by Pierce & Bickford at the same location in 1893.

Simply put, silk is made from the cocoon of the silkworm. Over a period of forty-eight hours, each silkworm extruded 1,000—1,300 yards of silken fiber until it was entirely enclosed in its cocoon. Four to six days later, the cocoons were treated to kill the chrysalis. Then gum from the cocoons had to be removed by soap and hot water. Finally, the much-wanted silk could be reeled. Multiple strands reeled together formed one silk thread, the size of a single human hair.

Two young women winding silk at the Sauquoit Silk Manufacturing Company of Philadelphia, March 27, 1918. Credit: Courtesy of the Pennsylvania State Archives.

Silk worm farms were started in the Allentown area but the endeavor involved more work than expected. Because of the silkworms extreme sensitivity to temperature and conditions, the cocoonery had to be kept at a constant 75 to 80 degrees, and the silkworms protected from drafts, tobacco smoke, thunder, and lightning.

Read & Lovatt is listed in the Elmira city directory as "silk throwsters." Silk throwing is the industrial process where silk that has been reeled into skeins, is cleaned, receives a twist and is wound onto bobbins. The yarn is twisted together with threads, in a process known as "doubling." At our factory, the silk "throwsters" or spinners prepared the material for the looms, and the output amounted to about 200,000 pounds annually.

The Read & Lovatt silk mills had many honors over the years, especially making the silk threads for the Inauguration Gown of Mrs. Theodore Roosevelt on January 13, 1905. Her gown was a vision in blue silk with birds woven in gold thread. To make sure that the first lady's dress was never copied, the pattern was destroyed upon completion. Read and Lovett also spun the silk used in the gown worn by Teddy Roosevelt's daughter, Alice Roosevelt Longworth, and inspired the popular song "Alice Blue Gown."

By 1912 Elmira's Read & Lovatt employed 250 and operated 40,000 spindles. A large addition in 1912 included two new boilers to power the spindles. A night shift provided the opportunity for women and girls to work day hours, and men and boys to work night hours.

Elmira's silk mill production peaked in the late 1920s. After that the Great Depression, increasing labor unrest, and competition from rayon began to affect the industry locally and nationally.

At some point around 1920 the name changed to the A & R Silk Mill. The mill eventually ceased operation in 1939 with only 60 employees. The mill was resurrected for a brief time by the Epstein Underwear Company of Scranton with 100 jobs, but did not last long.

Today, the silkworm moth lives only in captivity. Silkworms have been domesticated so that they can no longer survive independently in nature, particularly since they have lost the ability to fly. All wild populations are extinct, although presumably old relatives exist in Asia.

The Sisters of St. Joseph

by James Hare

SISTERS OF ST. JOSEPH SOON TO OPEN THEIR NEW HOSPITAL

Former School Thoroughly Equipped Institution For Charity Work—Catholic Women of City Will Endow a Free Bed—To Have a Meeting Tomorrow Night.

Headline in the Elmira *Star-Gazette* (Elmira, New York) · September 15, 1908 page 11.

Revend Mother Agnes Hines was concerned. The Sisters of St. Joseph were a teaching order, having never operated a hospital. She went to the chapel at the "Old Nazareth" and prayed that God would direct her and that the Holy Spirit would enlighten her to select the right Sister to head the daunting project. It came to Mother Agnes that, "the first Sister to enter the chapel to pray will be the one." Sister Rose Alice Conway was the next nun to pray at the chapel, and she would be the founder and first administrator of St. Joseph's Hospital until her death in 1939.

Sister Rose Alice and six other nuns opened the hospital on September 24, 1908. June 2014, marked the end of a very special relationship forged by the Sisters of St. Joseph with Elmira when Sister Marie Michael Miller, the last Sister of St. Joseph in Elmira returned to Rochester. She came to the city in 1946 as a nursing student at St. Joseph's. On the 100th anniversary of the founding of the hospital (September 24, 2009) the skilled nursing unit on the fifth floor was named the Marie Michael

Center. The plaque reads, "Beginning in 1950 Sister Marie Michael SSJ dedicated her life to caring for the patients and families at St. Joseph's...." Her departure will close a significant chapter in the history of our community.

The Sisters of St. Joseph was started in Le Puy, France on October 15, 1650. Their first charge was an orphanage. In 1834, the bishop of St. Louis asked the order to send missionary nuns to this country. Six sisters arrived in 1836. When Rochester became a diocese in 1868, the sisters, already at work in Canandaigua, were asked by Bishop Bernard J. McQuaid to devote themselves fully to the needs of the new diocese. Nazareth Convent was opened in 1871. From that year on the sisters were called upon to fill the teaching needs in the diocese which by 1893 amounted to 34 parochial schools.

In 1907, the title of the former Academy of Our Lady of the Angels on Market Street (St. Joseph Boulevard today) was transferred to the Congregation of the Sisters of St. Joseph for $10,000 because of the good work of John J. Hassett and Dr. Daniel P. Murphy among others. Sister Rose Alice and six other nuns came to Elmira to take charge of the new hospital. They went to local stores to purchase brooms, mops and pails. From the attic to the cellar they cleaned the old building of debris left by the workmen. That first night, exhausted by their labors they went to the St. Peter and Paul's convent. Sister Rose Alice hung her habit on the line to air and during the night it was stolen.

By the end of the first year of operation, St. Joseph's had 358 admissions, 31 births and only 14 deaths. The Sisters rose at 3AM to do laundry in the kitchen. After a day's work they returned to do the ironing. They made sure the patients had the best food possible even though they might diet on soup made from potato skins. In addition to regular nursing duties, the Sisters swept and cleaned the rooms and wards. When there was no electricity the lighting problem was solved by sticking a candle in a potato.

Support for the hospital came from dry goods stores donating sheets, soap and other useful items. The Ladies of St. Peter and Paul's conducted fruit and jelly showers while the Ladies of St. Mary's held musicales to raise funds. Every month two groups of Elmira matrons mended sheets and made towels for the hospital.

On October 2, 1908, the first student nurse, Miss Lena MacInerney, arrived. The Class of 1911 had four members. "Dating was taboo... and encountering a friend behind Sawyer's store was about the extent of the social life for the girls." The School of Nursing closed in 1988.

The Sisters of St. Joseph peaked in numbers at 40 in 1947. By 1996, Sister Marie Castagnaro (Administrator 1988-2010) noted, "fewer women are entering the convent and those who do are in their late 20's or older and already have careers." Marilyn Sullivan, who worked at St. Joseph's from 1977-1990 observed that, "there has always been an upbeat atmosphere there because the nuns were there. On days when work became stressful the difference between nuns and lay people was more apparent. The nuns calm demeanor was a comfort to patients... the nun's compassion came through to the patients...people trusted them."

Sister Marie Michael said, "I think our highest priority is to heal the total person... both the physical and the spiritual."

Men working on a telephone pole on the corner of State and East Market Streets, circa 1900. Photograph courtesy of the Eleanor Barnes Library.

Telegraphs and Telephones

by Diane Janowski

In 1846, Elmira was temporarily up-to-date. We had telegraph service thanks to Ezra Cornell who strung up a line from Ithaca to Elmira. Unfortunately, Elmirans did not use the new technology and Ezra, being a practical businessman, stopped the service after only a few months.

By 1847, Elmirans had a new working telegraph service running out of Hall's Book Store at 334 East Water Street run by Francis Hall. Mr. Hall was also Elmira's first express agent. Although Hall's telegraph was a convenience it was not always reliable – the wires easily fell off their poles during high winds. In 1850, another telegraph office opened over Dr. Paine's drug store on Water Street. The line ran from Elmira to Canandaigua and connected to the New York Central Railroad wires.

In 1852, an exclusive wire was strung for the Erie depot with an office in the American Hotel.

In 1855, Mr. Cornell connected lines between Addison and Newburgh with an office in Elmira. The Northern Central Railroad put up a line between Williamsport and Elmira with an office on Fifth Street.

The challenge for early telegraph service was that people only used them for emergencies and receipts barely covered expenses. Many small lines quickly went out of business.

In 1865, Western Union opened a new line from Buffalo to New York City with an office at the Brainard House on East Water Street. This enabled our regional newspapers to become members of the Associated Press. The telegraph provided "up to the minute" information. By this time, telegrams began making money.

In 1877, a local company connected forty telegraph boxes in hotels, offices, and private dwellings. This brought about a new occupation – telegraph operator. One needed to know Morse code to work the boxes. By 1879, telegrams to and from Elmira totaled around 200 per day. Wellsburg had two telegraph offices – one at the train depot and one at Morris Young's store. Horseheads, Lowman, and Ashland also had telegraph offices.

As we all know the telephone was invented by Alexander Graham Bell on March 1, 1876. Telephones were quickly recognized as a valuable utility and a stepping-stone to affluence. William N. Eastabrook was the first Elmiran to recognize these qualities. Easterbrook was a telegraph operator for the Northern Central Railroad. He was quick to sense that a voice through a wire would be a distinct improvement over Morse Code dots and dashes.

In late 1877, Elmira's first telephone was installed by Eastabrook in Jervis Langdon's office at 110 Baldwin Street. It connected to a telephone in the Western Union office at 150 Baldwin Street. He invited potential customers and prospective investors to visit to Langdon's office and learn how the technology might benefit their businesses. Eastabrook tried to interest his co-workers to invest $100 each with him and bring this new service to Elmira.

Frank E. Smith worked for Mr. Eastabrook at the railroad as a telegrapher. Along with Horace French, Sylvester French, and F. Ellery Fitch, they formed a partnership that launched the first telephone local company known as the Elmira Bell Telephone Exchange. Smith became the office manager and published the first local telephone book. Smith recalled in a 1936 *Star-Gazette* article, "The first telephone I remember was a clumsy oblong box-like contraption fastened to the wall and equipped with a little bell-lever."

By December 1879, enough Elmirans had subscribed to the idea of bringing service to our area. When telephone service finally connected Elmira to the world in 1880, forty-two customers had signed up - 36 businesses and 6 residences. The first telephone directory was quickly outdated as more and more customers subscribed. Businesses were the primary users of the service. They included A. B. Austin grocery store; Barker, Dounce & Rose hardware store; I. D. Booth hardware store; the Erie depot; the Park Church; and the "Reformatory." The first private residence to have the luxury of a telephone was the Jervis Langdon home on the corner of East Church and North Main Streets. Several lawyers also had residential telephones. By the end of 1881, the directory listed 191 numbers.

An Elmira *Gazette* ad in 1901:

"Wanted - One thousand chestnut telephone poles to be delivered at Elmira, New York. For particulars address the Elmira Telephone Company, No. 212 East Water Street."

Competing telephone companies erected their own poles and wires. Businesses required more than one telephone. A notice in the Elmira *Gazette* in 1902: "If you want to send in a want ad to the gazette you may use the telephone, either line. Call 396 on the old line or 286 on the new line."

Many residents resented the installation of telephone poles placed in front of their houses. From the Elmira *Gazette*, 1903: "Residents of the northern section of the city are complaining against the New York and Pennsylvania Telephone Company employees who are engaged in erecting new poles. Mrs. John Lonergan who resides at the corner of Washington Avenue and Magee Street compelled them to stop work by running out of the house and jumping into the freshly dug hole."

From the Elmira *Gazette*, 1904: *"The American Telephone and Telegraph Company, whose line runs from Montour Falls to Odessa, has been having all sorts of trouble lately. Several days ago, the inspector of the company made the discovery that about eight of their poles had been sawed into so that they were in imminent danger of falling to the ground."*

Many of us still recall when phone numbers increased from five digits to seven, adding the prefix "7-3" in 1958. This exchange was called "REgent" to help us remember.

Sources:

Elmira *Star-Gazette* March 4, 1936 p 16
Elmira *Gazette*
History of Tioga, Chemung, Tompkins, & Schuyler Counties. 1879
Towner, Ausburn. *Our County and Its People: A History of the Valley and County of Chemung, from the Closing Years of the Eighteenth Century 1892*

Wets vs Drys in Elmira

by James Hare

Elmira Is Voted "Bone Dry" By Overwhelming Majorities

Front page headline Elmira *Star-Gazette* April 18, 1918 page 1.

While World War I raged in Europe and General Pershing chased Pancho Villa in Mexico, there was a fierce debate in Elmira over whether the city should be "wet" or "dry." Elmira was considered the "cradle of the local option." While towns across New York State could vote on prohibition, cities could not. On April 16th and 17th, 1918 "the first two day municipal election in the history of America" was held in Elmira to resolve the issue.

Rachel Dworkin, Archivist at the Booth Library, Chemung County Historical Society, has noted that Elmira had a population of 37,176 in 1910. Folks could drink in 93 saloons, 33 hotels and 9 billiard halls. Liquor could also be purchased, "for medicinal purposes," at 27 drug stores. Much of the county was "dry" but Elmira was clearly "wet."

The Elmira *Herald* would claim that the fight to make Elmira "the first dry city of the third class in NYS" officially began when the Common Council adopted the Local Option on February 21, 1916 by a 7-5 vote. The council had been presented with a petition listing over 4,000 signatures in support of the resolution. However, those presenting the petition refused to make the signers names public. The *Herald* reported that "there was much comedy" at the council meeting over whether or not to accept the petition. Eventually names were reviewed in executive session but never published. Once passed the Local Option resolution was forwarded to the state legislature accompanied by a delegation of Elmirans. Bills were introduced in the state assembly and senate but local assemblyman Dr. R. P. Bush of Horseheads refused to support it, characterizing proponents of dry legislation as, "skunks and hyenas, as fakirs and character assassins as hypocrites and forgers, as self righteous, intolerant and spiteful." A hearing was held in Albany at which the "wets" presented their own petition (the dry petition was never presented) with over 5,000 signatures and about 60 people spoke. The *Telegram* reported that, "the Elmira local option bill is causing considerable discussion."

The bill did not pass in 1916 but did eventually along with the Brown Liquor Tax Law. The Brown Law allowed cities more control over licensing. In October 1917, the *Herald* reported the "Common Council played a little game of freeze out... with retail liquor dealers... It set aside practically all the business district and all of the central residential section of the city as a zone with which no additional liquor licenses can be obtained and within which there can be no further transfer of licenses." As a result 49 establishments (16 hotels, 33 saloons) lost their licenses. Referring to the loss of license revenue, prohibition activist Milo Shanks said, "I prefer a dead dry town to a dead drunk town."

If Mark Twain had been alive he might have retold a story he told in 1895 to an audience in New Zealand where a prohibitory law was under consideration.

> *"If prohibition came to town they could expect difficulties. He told them that in America a few years before, a stranger came to a dry town and discovered that the only place he could get a drink was at the pharmacy. When he asked the pharmacist for a drink, he found he needed a doctor's prescription except for snakebite. The man said where's the snake? The apothecary gave him the snake's address and he went off. Soon after, however, he came back and said, 'For goodness sake give me a drink.' That snake is engaged for months ahead."*

Elmira's opportunity to exercise the local option came in April 1918. There was much excitement as women would be allowed to vote if they registered. Nearly 12,000 did register with women outnumbering men 11,849 to 10,133.

Heated debate swept the city. The Elmira *Herald* was "wet," The Elmira *Advertiser* and *Star-Gazette* were "dry." President Lincoln's name was used by both sides. Mrs. Mary Armour, the "Georgia Whirlwind" spoke at the Colonial Theater claiming "human and political slavery" is what the liquor traffic demands not personal liberty." Advertising addressed to "Patriotic Drinkers" read, "Help win the war quickly! Do your share. Put your booze money into bonds." On the other hand it was argued that "prohibition is a menace to war activities." Congressman Jacob Meeker told a Colonial audience to "get behind Wilson and stop stirring up dissension and strife." The *Herald* observed that "bone-dry means higher taxes" and that the "last act of the Czar of Russia was the edict which interfered with the drink of his people..."

Out of 22,000 eligible voters, 20,402 voted. Elmira became "Bone-Dry" by a margin of 7,497 votes. Folks would not be able to get a drink even with a prescription. Thirty-eight cities across the state voted and twenty voted to be "dry." "The Noble Experiment," as Prohibition was called, became effective on January 16, 1920 and it was repealed December 5, 1933. During that period, in the words of former County Historian Tom Bryne , our area became "The Thirsty Tiers." Elmira had a two-year head start.

The Vin Fiz visits Elmira

by Diane Janowski

The *Vin Fiz* leaving Sheepshead Bay, September 17, 1911. Image courtesy of Diane Janowski.

On September 11, 1911, the Elmira *Star-Gazette* reported that:

"C. F Rodgers, the young aviator backed by Ogden Armour [of hot dog fame], will pass over Elmira the last of this week on his record breaking aeroplane flight from New York to Chicago. If things go right, Rodgers should reach this city the second or third day out of New York. In all probability he will make a stop in Elmira, whether or not he spends the night here."

"Vin Fiz" was the name of a new grape-flavored soft drink and was hailed by its company as "refreshing and invigorating." The new product, however, presented one large marketing problem – it tasted terrible. The company needed a very special strategy if they were to sell their product and came up with a novel idea to boost its popularity.

About eleven months earlier, publishing magnate William Randolph Hearst offered $50,000 to the fastest aviator to cross the country coast-to-coast within thirty days. With Hearst's contest, Vin Fiz had its gimmick. Early in this contest, several aviators tried, but the task proved too difficult. Even nine years after the Wright brothers first successfully flew, airplanes were still considered impractical and a novelty. These early airplanes flew at levels lower than the tops of our hills, had no radios, could only fly in good weather, and broke down on almost every flight.

In September 1911, three aviators announced their intentions to try the stunt. Hearst set no specific route - just to fly from ocean to ocean. Pilot Robert Fowler chose to fly from California to New York, while pilots Jimmy Ward and Vin Fiz's Calbraith Perry Rodgers were to fly from New York to California. Fowler took off in California on September 11. Ward left Governor's Island, New York on September 13, and Rodgers left Sheepshead Bay, New York on September 17. Rodgers' aircraft was decorated with the Vin Fiz trademark and, in addition to the prize money, should he win it, Rodgers was to receive from Armour $5 for every mile flown with his aircraft so lettered.

Robert Fowler crashed on his first day in the California mountains, but he vowed to continue. After a week of crashes, he finally became discouraged and quit. Meanwhile, Jimmy Ward planned to follow the Erie Railroad line through New York, but at Jersey City, New Jersey, was confused and started following the Lehigh Valley Railroad line. When he realized his mistake, he retraced his route to Jersey City, found the correct railroad line, and headed toward Middletown, New York where 6,000 fans were waiting. On his second day, the wire service out of Port Jervis, New York reported, "Never before in the history of Neversink and the Delaware River Valley has any single event caused as much excitement and interest as the flight of Aviator Ward, who is bound from the Atlantic to the Pacific coast." At this point, the weather turned bad and he was stuck in Callicoon for two days, missing his fly-over at the fair at Owego, New York. On the fourth day, Ward flew over Binghamton at 2:45 PM, but soon developed mechanical difficulties, and landed at Owego. When he left Owego on the fifth day, someone was supposed to telephone Elmira to say that he was coming, but before the call came, Ward was already here. A few people reported seeing him fly over Elmira at 11:15AM, and shortly thereafter, his bearings burned out and he was forced to land on Rose Hill in Corning. Repairs took almost three days. On the eighth day, he took off, but soon crashed in farmer Benjamin Lynch's cornfield near Addison. Farmer Lynch threatened to sue for his damaged corn, but changed his mind the next day. Ward claimed he had a jinx on his plane. Ward eventually had to abandon the challenge because his funds ran out.

Thirty-two year old Calbraith Perry Rodgers had less than sixty hours of flying experience when he left New York on September 17, in a Wright brothers' type EX spruce, wire, and fabric bi-plane with a 35 horsepower, 4-cylinder engine. Cal's plane followed a special Vin Fiz train. The passenger car, with its top painted white, served as his beacon. Rodgers' wife, Mabel, his cousin, Lt. John Rodgers, Crew Chief Charles Taylor, and other members of the crew occupied the other cars. The special car was dubbed the "white hangar," and provided a first aid center, and machine shop with spare parts and tools. Rumor suggested it carried a coffin too, "just in case."

Elmira was on Cal's route and spotters on the Lake Street bridge first saw the *Vin Fiz* after 5:00 PM on September 22. At first, he was just a speck in the southern sky, but as he neared, he was flying so low that the words "Vin Fiz" were clearly readable.

When Rodgers got to Elmira, he flew over the city looking for the Chemung County fairgrounds, as it was a good place to land. He saw nothing that looked like it, and doubled back. He saw his train near the Elmira Bridge Works (between Miller and Home Streets). It had been sideswiped by a freight train, but sustained no serious damage. In an effort to get to his train, he landed in the first field that he came to. It was farmer Edmund

Miller's open meadow (now McNaught Field near Miller's Pond) at 5:55 PM. Both the *Star-Gazette* and the Elmira *Advertiser* said that his landing was "graceful." Rodgers was then taken "to the city" in an automobile to the Hotel Rathbun where his crew had gathered.

The airplane was roped off for the night. The next morning, spectators began gathering early, and by 8:30 AM the meadow "looked like a county fair." After making some minor repairs, several thousand Elmirans watched Rodgers take off at 2:15 PM.

Rodgers continued his journey through New York State, west to Illinois, south to Texas, and finally west toward California. Weather and machinery failure cost him any hope of winning the prize. He was in Oklahoma when the prize date expired, but he continued to fulfill his contract with Armour. Rodgers had his share of problems, in Texas where he admitted he had spent more time on the ground than in the air.

The *Vin Fiz* was the first airplane ever seen in many of his stops or crashes. Elmira was slightly more sophisticated than the rest of the country because two months earlier the city witnessed Lincoln Beachey's bi-plane. In Austin, Texas, 3,000 spectators came out to see their first airplane. On October 17, 1911, the *Vin Fiz* became the first airplane seen in Denison, Texas. Rodgers landed in a field near Denison to refuel his plane after dropping little pink leaflets advertising Vin Fiz. He then lost his way and went nearly to Wichita Falls before he corrected his direction and headed for Fort Worth. He did finish his contract with Armour and became the first man to fly across the continent. Cal Rodgers utilized forty-nine days to travel 3,350 miles. He made sixty-nine stops and crash-landed nineteen times, and the poor *Vin Fiz* was rebuilt four times. He ended the first transcontinental flight by landing in Tournament Park (now on the Cal Tech campus) in Pasadena, California.

Even though Cal made it to California, he felt his journey was not complete until the *Vin Fiz* actually touched the Pacific Ocean. On November 12, he left Long Beach, but was forced to land. On December 10, he tried and succeeded by landing on the beach and taxiing into the water.

A few months later, Rodgers was "chasing sea gulls" when one bird became caught in the rudder wire, and while trying to extricate the bird, the wire broke and the plane crashed into the Pacific Ocean killing Rodgers. In 1934, the rebuilt *Vin Fiz* joined the collection of the Smithsonian Institute in Washington, D.C.

Calbraith Perry Rodgers was inducted into the National Aviation Hall of Fame in 1964.

Sources:

Elmira *Advertiser*, September 11-30, 1911.
Elmira *Star-Gazette*, September 11-30, 1911.
http://caltech.edu/matchi/pasadena.html
http://nasm.edu/nasm/aero/aircraft/

Christian Science in Elmira

by James Hare

MANY HEARD
THE LECTURE

—

Arthur R. Vosburgh Discussed
Christian Science and Its Work.

—

CHRISTIANITY CERTAIN SCIENCE

Headline from Elmira *Daily Gazette and Free Press*, November 15 1904, page 8.

It was an important day for the First Church of Christ Scientist in Elmira. The Elmira *Advertiser,* November 15, 1904 reported that, "500 or more persons" had gathered at the Park Church the previous evening to hear Arthur R. Vosburgh C.S.B. of Rochester give, "the first lecture ever given under the auspices of Christian Scientists of this city." Vosburgh was former Presbyterian minister who had become a member of the Christian Science board of lectureship of the First Church of Christ, Scientist of Boston, Massachusetts.

According to the *Advertiser*, the lectureship was one of the educational branches of the Christian Science Church. Each individual church tries to have at least one lecture each year.

The *Sunday Telegram* (March 13, 1966) noted that, "interest in Christian Science in Elmira dates back to 1891." It was not until ten years later, on Wednesday evening, March 6, 1901, that eight believers met at the home of Mr. and Mrs. George Lawrence at 625 West Water Street "to consider the advisability of holding public services." The decision was to begin activities at once, and the first public service was held at the Lawrence home the following Sunday evening.

The Christian Science Church was founded by Mary Baker Eddy. Martin Gardner quotes from her autobiography in his book, *The Healing Revolution of Mary Baker Eddy*:

> *"It was in Massachusetts, in the year 1866, that I discovered the Science of Divine Metaphysical Healing, which I afterwards named Christian Science. The discovery came to pass in this way. During twenty years prior to my discovery, I had been trying to trace all physical effects to a mental cause; and in the latter part of 1866 I gained the Scientific (sic) certainty that all causation was Mind (sic) and every effect a mental phenomenon.*
>
> *My immediate recovery from the effects of an injury, caused by an accident, an injury that neither medicine nor surgery could reach, was the falling apple that led me to the discovering how to be well myself, and how to make others so...."*

In April, 1901 the meeting place for the local Christian Science Church moved from the Lawrence home to Warner Hall at 219 West Gray Street and in October 1902 to Bryant Hall school building at 214 West Gray Street. On December 6, 1902 the church was formally organized with eight charter members and "incorporated under the laws of the State of New York." The church changed location in March 1905, moving to the Railroad Y.M.C.A. building at the corner of Railroad Avenue and Church Street.

In 1908, it moved once again to the hall over the Elmira Arms Company. In 1909, a generous offer of financial support enabled the church to purchase the former Bryant Hall at 214 West Gray Street.

In 1924, the Christian Science Church purchased the Diven home on the corner of West Church and Walnut Streets. The four-story, nineteen-room building had been constructed in 1867 by Eugene Diven becoming one of the grand homes in Elmira. The church members were excited by this opportunity to grow, moving in after renovations in 1926. Church services continued in that building up to and after the Agnes Flood in 1972. A huge fire in October 1973, ravaged the building and a decision was made to build a new house of worship.

The First Presbyterian Church offered its building to the Christian Science congregation until a new church was built. On Sunday, July 18, 1976 the new church opened its doors. The building, designed by Louis Jensen of New York City, and built by the West Hill Construction Company has an octagon shape.

A member of the church since 1946, has remarked that "these are stalwart people." Except for an occasional blizzard, services have been held every Wednesday and Sunday despite two World Wars, the 1972 flood and the fire in 1973. She went on to say, "We get here by hook or by crook."

"You Will Like Elmira"

by Diane Janowski

I was born in St. Joseph's Hospital in 1960. I like to think back to the time, half a century before, when Elmira was a dramatically different landscape. Horses and wagons were the primary source of transportation. They held the very first

MEET YOUR FRIENDS
at
GULKA'S
POLISH VILLAGE
900 Lackawanna Ave.

Polish Village restaurant advertisement, Elmira *Star-Gazette* December 23, 1960, page 11.

auto show in Elmira at the New York State Armory on Church Street. George M. Diven had purchased a 1910 REO from the LaFrance Motor Company. Before 1910, downtown had been centered around Lake and East Water Streets. Retail businesses, offices, and small manufacturers had built westward toward Main Street.

Mark Twain passed away and was buried at Woodlawn Cemetery. 1910 seems like a very long time ago. Now, I have lived more than half a century since I was born, and what a difference that has made.

The **1960 Elmira City Directory** described Elmira as a vibrant center. "It dominates the region for many miles as the trade, industrial, financial and transportation hub of the Southern Tier. Each industry has ample space to expand and new sites are strategically located to all facilities. The proximity of raw materials gives added impetus to Elmira's commercial life... 119 miles from anthracite coal, 50 miles from bituminous coal and 55 miles from the Pennsylvania oil fields."

Elmira had about 75 industries employing over 17,000 persons. The big ones included: American LaFrance, Sperry Rand, Kennedy Valve, Thatcher Glass, Ward LaFrance, Chemung Foundry, Hardinge, Hilliard, F. M. Howell, Artistic Card, General Electric, Moore Business Forms, National Homes, Schweizer Aircraft, Eclipse, and American Bridge.

Elmira was the fifteenth largest city in New York State with a population of 52,300. Chemung County had a population of over 93,000 and we were still growing.

The City Directory cited Elmira as one of the most prosperous commercial sectors of the Eastern U.S. with "676 retail stores, 88 wholesale houses, and 675 professional offices." We enjoyed five off-street free parking lots.

In 1960, women frequented 82 beauty shops like the Fashionette Beauty Shop on Jefferson Street, American Beauty Parlor and Mineral Baths on Park Place, and Midge's, and Millie's, both on Riverside Avenue. Men could choose from 50 barbershops like Ace on Luce Street, Ideal on Water Street, or Sanitary Barber Shop, also on Water Street.

If you father gave you your 50¢ allowance (worth about $4 today), you could venture downtown and consider from many enticements. The Karmelkorn Shop sounds good, or The Astor on East Water offered ice cream and candies. There were Caparulo's on Clinton Street, Mr. Peanut at the corner of Main and Water, Doc's Candies on Hoffman Street, and Uncle Tom's on Davis.

Toy stores abounded: Bunis Toys & Hobbies, and Kids Stuff on East Water, Elmira Arms Company on North Main, and White's Toyland on Pennsylvania Ave. Just for fun you could shop for all kinds of things at W. T. Grant, J. J. Newbury, Kresge's, Woolworth's, or the two Army & Navy surplus stores, Winnick's and Harold's.

There were over a dozen liquor stores in or near downtown Elmira, including Family Liquor on Lake Street, and Ace, Bush, and Shappee's, all on East Water Street. Mom and Dad could treat each other to jewelry at Alpert's, Deister & Butler, Dozack, Drake's, Furman, Ray's, Schoonover's, Shreibman's, Siskin, Smith, Swartout, and Winklestein's, all downtown.

Fashionable clothing stores included Rosenbaum's, the Gorton Coy, Cameo Shop, Richard's, Markson's, Sportogs, Werdenberg's, and H. Strauss. After you had tried on enough clothes, you could head for the Tea Room in the basement of Iszard's for coffee and a slice of their delicious brown bread.

Up at Sears & Roebuck the whole family could be satisfied with clothes, tools, toys, and roasted peanuts.

SCHANAKER'S
Stream-Lined Diner
Never Too Late at Schanaker's—We're Always Open!

107 State St.   Elmira, N. Y.

FREE PARKING IN THE REAR WHILE YOU DINE ONLY

Schanaker's advertisement Elmira *Star-Gazette* July 10, 1941, page 7.

After a hard day of shopping, your family had plenty of dining-out options. Within the city limits, Elmira supported 145 restaurants. For a formal evening (especially senior proms), we went to the Mark Twain Hotel. If we wanted Italian fare, we had Moretti's, Mustico's, Lib's, Lag's, Manzari's, and The Palms. And here are some of the more obscure choices: Elmira Chuck Wagon, Blackies East Side Lunch, and Manhattan Restaurant all on East Water; Mambo Club on North Main; The Hy-Boy Drive-In on Baldwin; N-Joy-N-Eat on South Main; New Beaux Arts Grill on Carroll; Oasis Restaurant on State; and the Polish Village on Lackawanna Ave. Elmira's famous diners were Schanaker's, Clinton, Colonial, City Line, Elite, Elmira, Lawrence, and Vic's.

Elmirans enjoyed 340 acres of city parks. Our largest park in 1960 was Eldridge Park with 63 acres. Newtown Battlefield was a state park. The Strathmont estate was a tourist attraction "representing the roaring 20s." Arnot Art Gallery, Steele Memorial Library, and the Chemung County Historical Society stood out amongst the group of cultural attractions.

From the *1960 City Directory*:

> *"The visitor in our midst soon feels the warmth and friendliness of the American way of living and working together. He is always welcome, for him we say – "You Will Like Elmira."*

Source:

Manning's Elmira City Directory, 1960

Elmira's Melting Pot

by Diane Janowski

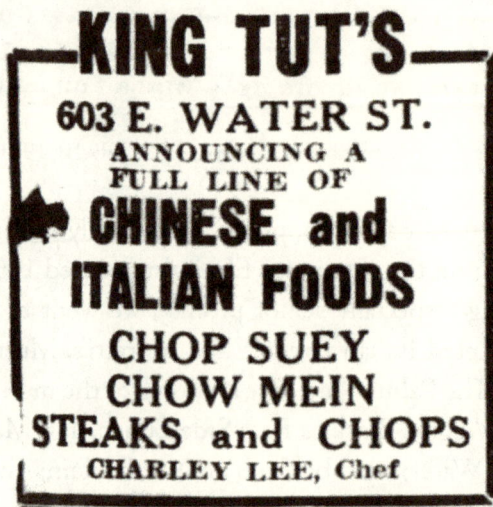

KING TUT'S

603 E. WATER ST.
ANNOUNCING A
FULL LINE OF

CHINESE and ITALIAN FOODS

CHOP SUEY
CHOW MEIN
STEAKS and CHOPS
CHARLEY LEE, Chef

Ad in the *Star-Gazette* (Elmira, New York) November 4, 1939, page 9.

Elmira's first wave of immigrants came from Ireland after the American Revolution. Three of the earliest were John and William Fitzsimmons, and Abijah Ward. They came seeking business opportunities between 1790 and 1820. The first known Irish businesses included a sawmill, a blacksmith shop, and The Telegraph newspaper. Irish laborers helped to produce linen and wool cloth in early Elmira.

Between 1820 and 1860, Irishmen came and worked as skilled laborers and mechanics. They helped dig the Chemung Canal, and lay tracks for the Erie Railroad. They helped at the Rolling Mill on Washington Avenue, and in the railroad shops. By the 1890s, the Irish had become prominent in politics, industry, law enforcement, and fire prevention.

The first person of German descent in this area was Matthias Hollenback, who began a trading post around 1790. Germans began arriving here in 1848, and again in 1871 after the Franco-Prussian War. In

1915, anti-German sentiment forced Elmira's protestant German church to switch its practice of giving sermons from its native language to English. Elmira's Germans found employment as musicians, farmers, bakers, contractors, and restaurateurs.

Jews began settling in Elmira around 1848. They came as peddlers bringing jewelry and other luxuries. As they became more prosperous they opened stores. Early Jewish businesses include bakeries, barbershops, groceries, butcher shops, cigar and carriage factories, and clothing shops. They prospered as physicians, lawyers, and merchants.

African Americans migrated to this area, many as slaves, fugitive slaves, or free blacks. Some used Elmira as a "stop" on their way to Canada. Others found Elmira friendly and settled here. They found employment as masons, shoemakers, grocers, and barbers.

By 1910, hundreds of Polish families had settled in Elmira, and followed occupations such as tailors, grocers, bakers, restaurateurs, and contractors.

Ukrainians settled in Elmira Heights between 1895 and 1905. They easily found employment in the local knitting mills, the Rolling Mill, the Elmira Bridge Works, and the Eclipse plant.

The Italians were the last large group to arrive in Elmira. They came between 1886 and 1910. Italians found jobs as restaurateurs, railroad workers, contractors, laborers, carpenters, bakers, grocers, shoemakers, and barbers.

The Greeks came to Elmira after 1900. Many had goals of owning their own businesses. Soon Elmira had Greek-owned candy stores, restaurants, flower shops, cleaning establishments, and shoeshine parlors.

The 2000 Chemung County census shows Elmira's residents to be of English, African-American, Asian, German, Hispanic/Latino, Irish, Italian, Native American, or Polish descent.

Today, well-educated and highly specialized immigrants come to Elmira seeking jobs in fields that their ancestors never envisioned, including high-tech, medical, and engineering fields.

About the authors and this book....

Diane Janowski is the current Elmira City historian. She is also the editor of *New York History Review*, and was formerly the editor of the *Chemung Historical Journal*.

   She has written many books about Elmira and Chemung County history, and co-authored the book *Images of America, The Chemung Valley* with Allen C. Smith.

James Hare is a retired teacher of American History and Government from the Elmira City School District. He is also a former mayor and councilman for the City of Elmira.

   He co-authored the book *Images of America, Elmira* with former county historian J. Arthur Kieffer.

Hare and Janowski are freelance writers for the Elmira *Star-Gazette*. Since 2014, they each write monthly articles on the history of the city of Elmira, New York. This book is a selection of their articles.

Be sure to look for our first book!

TRUE STORIES
of Elmira, New York

Volume 1

By James Hare & Diane Janowski